FREE Study Skills DVD Offer

Dear Customer,

Thank you for your purchase from Mometrix! We consider it an honor and privilege that you have purchased our product and want to ensure your satisfaction.

As a way of showing our appreciation and to help us better serve you, we have developed a Study Skills DVD that we would like to give you for FREE. **This DVD covers our "best practices" for studying for your exam, from using our study materials to preparing for the day of the test.**

All that we ask is that you email us your feedback that would describe your experience so far with our product. Good, bad or indifferent, we want to know what you think!

To get your **FREE Study Skills DVD**, email freedvd@mometrix.com with "FREE STUDY SKILLS DVD" in the subject line and the following information in the body of the email:

a. The name of the product you purchased.

b. Your product rating on a scale of 1-5, with 5 being the highest rating.

c. Your feedback. It can be long, short, or anything in-between, just your impressions and experience so far with our product. Good feedback might include how our study material met your needs and will highlight features of the product that you found helpful.

d. Your full name and shipping address where you would like us to send your free DVD.

If you have any questions or concerns, please don't hesitate to contact me directly.

Thanks again!

Sincerely,

Jay Willis
Vice President
jay.willis@mometrix.com
1-800-673-8175

Virginia

SOL Earth Science

Virginia SOL Test Review for the
Virginia Standards of Learning
End of Course Exams

Dear Future Exam Success Story:

First of all, **THANK YOU** for purchasing Mometrix study materials!

Second, congratulations! You are one of the few determined test-takers who are committed to doing whatever it takes to excel on your exam. **You have come to the right place.** We developed these study materials with one goal in mind: to deliver you the information you need in a format that's concise and easy to use.

In addition to optimizing your guide for the content of the test, we've outlined our recommended steps for breaking down the preparation process into small, attainable goals so you can make sure you stay on track.

We've also analyzed the entire test-taking process, identifying the most common pitfalls and showing how you can overcome them and be ready for any curveball the test throws you.

Standardized testing is one of the biggest obstacles on your road to success, which only increases the importance of doing well in the high-pressure, high-stakes environment of test day. Your results on this test could have a significant impact on your future, and this guide provides the information and practical advice to help you achieve your full potential on test day.

Your success is our success

We would love to hear from you! If you would like to share the story of your exam success or if you have any questions or comments in regard to our products, please contact us at **800-673-8175** or **support@mometrix.com**.

Thanks again for your business and we wish you continued success!

Sincerely,
The Mometrix Test Preparation Team

Need more help? Check out our flashcards at: http://MometrixFlashcards.com/SOL

Written and edited by the Mometrix Exam Secrets Test Prep Team
Printed in the United States of America

TABLE OF CONTENTS

Introduction

Thank you for purchasing this resource! You have made the choice to prepare yourself for a test that could have a huge impact on your future, and this guide is designed to help you be fully ready for test day. Obviously, it's important to have a solid understanding of the test material, but you also need to be prepared for the unique environment and stressors of the test, so that you can perform to the best of your abilities.

For this purpose, the first section that appears in this guide is the **Secret Keys**. We've devoted countless hours to meticulously researching what works and what doesn't, and we've boiled down our findings to the five most impactful steps you can take to improve your performance on the test. We start at the beginning with study planning and move through the preparation process, all the way to the testing strategies that will help you get the most out of what you know when you're finally sitting in front of the test.

We recommend that you start preparing for your test as far in advance as possible. However, if you've bought this guide as a last-minute study resource and only have a few days before your test, we recommend that you skip over the first two Secret Keys since they address a long-term study plan.

If you struggle with **test anxiety**, we strongly encourage you to check out our recommendations for how you can overcome it. Test anxiety is a formidable foe, but it can be beaten, and we want to make sure you have the tools you need to defeat it.

Secret Key #1 – Plan Big, Study Small

There's a lot riding on your performance. If you want to ace this test, you're going to need to keep your skills sharp and the material fresh in your mind. You need a plan that lets you review everything you need to know while still fitting in your schedule. We'll break this strategy down into three categories.

Information Organization

Start with the information you already have: the official test outline. From this, you can make a complete list of all the concepts you need to cover before the test. Organize these concepts into groups that can be studied together, and create a list of any related vocabulary you need to learn so you can brush up on any difficult terms. You'll want to keep this vocabulary list handy once you actually start studying since you may need to add to it along the way.

Time Management

Once you have your set of study concepts, decide how to spread them out over the time you have left before the test. Break your study plan into small, clear goals so you have a manageable task for each day and know exactly what you're doing. Then just focus on one small step at a time. When you manage your time this way, you don't need to spend hours at a time studying. Studying a small block of content for a short period each day helps you retain information better and avoid stressing over how much you have left to do. You can relax knowing that you have a plan to cover everything in time. In order for this strategy to be effective though, you have to start studying early and stick to your schedule. Avoid the exhaustion and futility that comes from last-minute cramming!

Study Environment

The environment you study in has a big impact on your learning. Studying in a coffee shop, while probably more enjoyable, is not likely to be as fruitful as studying in a quiet room. It's important to keep distractions to a minimum. You're only planning to study for a short block of time, so make the most of it. Don't pause to check your phone or get up to find a snack. It's also important to **avoid multitasking**. Research has consistently shown that multitasking will make your studying dramatically less effective. Your study area should also be comfortable and well-lit so you don't have the distraction of straining your eyes or sitting on an uncomfortable chair.

The time of day you study is also important. You want to be rested and alert. Don't wait until just before bedtime. Study when you'll be most likely to comprehend and remember. Even better, if you know what time of day your test will be, set that time aside for study. That way your brain will be used to working on that subject at that specific time and you'll have a better chance of recalling information.

Finally, it can be helpful to team up with others who are studying for the same test. Your actual studying should be done in as isolated an environment as possible, but the work of organizing the information and setting up the study plan can be divided up. In between study sessions, you can discuss with your teammates the concepts that you're all studying and quiz each other on the details. Just be sure that your teammates are as serious about the test as you are. If you find that your study time is being replaced with social time, you might need to find a new team.

Secret Key #2 – Make Your Studying Count

You're devoting a lot of time and effort to preparing for this test, so you want to be absolutely certain it will pay off. This means doing more than just reading the content and hoping you can remember it on test day. It's important to make every minute of study count. There are two main areas you can focus on to make your studying count:

Retention

It doesn't matter how much time you study if you can't remember the material. You need to make sure you are retaining the concepts. To check your retention of the information you're learning, try recalling it at later times with minimal prompting. Try carrying around flashcards and glance at one or two from time to time or ask a friend who's also studying for the test to quiz you.

To enhance your retention, look for ways to put the information into practice so that you can apply it rather than simply recalling it. If you're using the information in practical ways, it will be much easier to remember. Similarly, it helps to solidify a concept in your mind if you're not only reading it to yourself but also explaining it to someone else. Ask a friend to let you teach them about a concept you're a little shaky on (or speak aloud to an imaginary audience if necessary). As you try to summarize, define, give examples, and answer your friend's questions, you'll understand the concepts better and they will stay with you longer. Finally, step back for a big picture view and ask yourself how each piece of information fits with the whole subject. When you link the different concepts together and see them working together as a whole, it's easier to remember the individual components.

Finally, practice showing your work on any multi-step problems, even if you're just studying. Writing out each step you take to solve a problem will help solidify the process in your mind, and you'll be more likely to remember it during the test.

Modality

Modality simply refers to the means or method by which you study. Choosing a study modality that fits your own individual learning style is crucial. No two people learn best in exactly the same way, so it's important to know your strengths and use them to your advantage.

For example, if you learn best by visualization, focus on visualizing a concept in your mind and draw an image or a diagram. Try color-coding your notes, illustrating them, or creating symbols that will trigger your mind to recall a learned concept. If you learn best by hearing or discussing information, find a study partner who learns the same way or read aloud to yourself. Think about how to put the information in your own words. Imagine that you are giving a lecture on the topic and record yourself so you can listen to it later.

For any learning style, flashcards can be helpful. Organize the information so you can take advantage of spare moments to review. Underline key words or phrases. Use different colors for different categories. Mnemonic devices (such as creating a short list in which every item starts with the same letter) can also help with retention. Find what works best for you and use it to store the information in your mind most effectively and easily.

Secret Key #3 – Practice the Right Way

Your success on test day depends not only on how many hours you put into preparing, but also on whether you prepared the right way. It's good to check along the way to see if your studying is paying off. One of the most effective ways to do this is by taking practice tests to evaluate your progress. Practice tests are useful because they show exactly where you need to improve. Every time you take a practice test, pay special attention to these three groups of questions:

- The questions you got wrong
- The questions you had to guess on, even if you guessed right
- The questions you found difficult or slow to work through

This will show you exactly what your weak areas are, and where you need to devote more study time. Ask yourself why each of these questions gave you trouble. Was it because you didn't understand the material? Was it because you didn't remember the vocabulary? Do you need more repetitions on this type of question to build speed and confidence? Dig into those questions and figure out how you can strengthen your weak areas as you go back to review the material.

Additionally, many practice tests have a section explaining the answer choices. It can be tempting to read the explanation and think that you now have a good understanding of the concept. However, an explanation likely only covers part of the question's broader context. Even if the explanation makes sense, **go back and investigate** every concept related to the question until you're positive you have a thorough understanding.

As you go along, keep in mind that the practice test is just that: practice. Memorizing these questions and answers will not be very helpful on the actual test because it is unlikely to have any of the same exact questions. If you only know the right answers to the sample questions, you won't be prepared for the real thing. **Study the concepts** until you understand them fully, and then you'll be able to answer any question that shows up on the test.

It's important to wait on the practice tests until you're ready. If you take a test on your first day of study, you may be overwhelmed by the amount of material covered and how much you need to learn. Work up to it gradually.

On test day, you'll need to be prepared for answering questions, managing your time, and using the test-taking strategies you've learned. It's a lot to balance, like a mental marathon that will have a big impact on your future. Like training for a marathon, you'll need to start slowly and work your way up. When test day arrives, you'll be ready.

Start with the strategies you've read in the first two Secret Keys—plan your course and study in the way that works best for you. If you have time, consider using multiple study resources to get different approaches to the same concepts. It can be helpful to see difficult concepts from more than one angle. Then find a good source for practice tests. Many times, the test website will suggest potential study resources or provide sample tests.

Practice Test Strategy

When you're ready to start taking practice tests, follow this strategy:

Untimed and Open-Book Practice

Take the first test with no time constraints and with your notes and study guide handy. Take your time and focus on applying the strategies you've learned.

Timed and Open-Book Practice

Take the second practice test open-book as well, but set a timer and practice pacing yourself to finish in time.

Timed and Closed-Book Practice

Take any other practice tests as if it were test day. Set a timer and put away your study materials. Sit at a table or desk in a quiet room, imagine yourself at the testing center, and answer questions as quickly and accurately as possible.

Keep repeating timed and closed-book tests on a regular basis until you run out of practice tests or it's time for the actual test. Your mind will be ready for the schedule and stress of test day, and you'll be able to focus on recalling the material you've learned.

Secret Key #4 – Pace Yourself

Once you're fully prepared for the material on the test, your biggest challenge on test day will be managing your time. Just knowing that the clock is ticking can make you panic even if you have plenty of time left. Work on pacing yourself so you can build confidence against the time constraints of the exam. Pacing is a difficult skill to master, especially in a high-pressure environment, so **practice is vital**.

Set time expectations for your pace based on how much time is available. For example, if a section has 60 questions and the time limit is 30 minutes, you know you have to average 30 seconds or less per question in order to answer them all. Although 30 seconds is the hard limit, set 25 seconds per question as your goal, so you reserve extra time to spend on harder questions. When you budget extra time for the harder questions, you no longer have any reason to stress when those questions take longer to answer.

Don't let this time expectation distract you from working through the test at a calm, steady pace, but keep it in mind so you don't spend too much time on any one question. Recognize that taking extra time on one question you don't understand may keep you from answering two that you do understand later in the test. If your time limit for a question is up and you're still not sure of the answer, mark it and move on, and come back to it later if the time and the test format allow. If the testing format doesn't allow you to return to earlier questions, just make an educated guess; then put it out of your mind and move on.

On the easier questions, be careful not to rush. It may seem wise to hurry through them so you have more time for the challenging ones, but it's not worth missing one if you know the concept and just didn't take the time to read the question fully. Work efficiently but make sure you understand the question and have looked at all of the answer choices, since more than one may seem right at first.

Even if you're paying attention to the time, you may find yourself a little behind at some point. You should speed up to get back on track, but do so wisely. Don't panic; just take a few seconds less on each question until you're caught up. Don't guess without thinking, but do look through the answer choices and eliminate any you know are wrong. If you can get down to two choices, it is often worthwhile to guess from those. Once you've chosen an answer, move on and don't dwell on any that you skipped or had to hurry through. If a question was taking too long, chances are it was one of the harder ones, so you weren't as likely to get it right anyway.

On the other hand, if you find yourself getting ahead of schedule, it may be beneficial to slow down a little. The more quickly you work, the more likely you are to make a careless mistake that will affect your score. You've budgeted time for each question, so don't be afraid to spend that time. Practice an efficient but careful pace to get the most out of the time you have.

Secret Key #5 – Have a Plan for Guessing

When you're taking the test, you may find yourself stuck on a question. Some of the answer choices seem better than others, but you don't see the one answer choice that is obviously correct. What do you do?

The scenario described above is very common, yet most test takers have not effectively prepared for it. Developing and practicing a plan for guessing may be one of the single most effective uses of your time as you get ready for the exam.

In developing your plan for guessing, there are three questions to address:

- When should you start the guessing process?
- How should you narrow down the choices?
- Which answer should you choose?

When to Start the Guessing Process

Unless your plan for guessing is to select C every time (which, despite its merits, is not what we recommend), you need to leave yourself enough time to apply your answer elimination strategies. Since you have a limited amount of time for each question, that means that if you're going to give yourself the best shot at guessing correctly, you have to decide quickly whether or not you will guess.

Of course, the best-case scenario is that you don't have to guess at all, so first, see if you can answer the question based on your knowledge of the subject and basic reasoning skills. Focus on the key words in the question and try to jog your memory of related topics. Give yourself a chance to bring the knowledge to mind, but once you realize that you don't have (or you can't access) the knowledge you need to answer the question, it's time to start the guessing process.

It's almost always better to start the guessing process too early than too late. It only takes a few seconds to remember something and answer the question from knowledge. Carefully eliminating wrong answer choices takes longer. Plus, going through the process of eliminating answer choices can actually help jog your memory.

Summary: Start the guessing process as soon as you decide that you can't answer the question based on your knowledge.

How to Narrow Down the Choices

The next chapter in this book (**Test-Taking Strategies**) includes a wide range of strategies for how to approach questions and how to look for answer choices to eliminate. You will definitely want to read those carefully, practice them, and figure out which ones work best for you. Here though, we're going to address a mindset rather than a particular strategy.

Your chances of guessing an answer correctly depend on how many options you are choosing from.

How many choices you have	How likely you are to guess correctly
5	20%
4	25%
3	33%
2	50%
1	100%

You can see from this chart just how valuable it is to be able to eliminate incorrect answers and make an educated guess, but there are two things that many test takers do that cause them to miss out on the benefits of guessing:

- Accidentally eliminating the correct answer
- Selecting an answer based on an impression

We'll look at the first one here, and the second one in the next section.

To avoid accidentally eliminating the correct answer, we recommend a thought exercise called **the $5 challenge**. In this challenge, you only eliminate an answer choice from contention if you are willing to bet $5 on it being wrong. Why $5? Five dollars is a small but not insignificant amount of money. It's an amount you could afford to lose but wouldn't want to throw away. And while losing $5 once might not hurt too much, doing it twenty times will set you back $100. In the same way, each small decision you make—eliminating a choice here, guessing on a question there—won't by itself impact your score very much, but when you put them all together, they can make a big difference. By holding each answer choice elimination decision to a higher standard, you can reduce the risk of accidentally eliminating the correct answer.

The $5 challenge can also be applied in a positive sense: If you are willing to bet $5 that an answer choice *is* correct, go ahead and mark it as correct.

Summary: Only eliminate an answer choice if you are willing to bet $5 that it is wrong.

Which Answer to Choose

You're taking the test. You've run into a hard question and decided you'll have to guess. You've eliminated all the answer choices you're willing to bet $5 on. Now you have to pick an answer. Why do we even need to talk about this? Why can't you just pick whichever one you feel like when the time comes?

The answer to these questions is that if you don't come into the test with a plan, you'll rely on your impression to select an answer choice, and if you do that, you risk falling into a trap. The test writers know that everyone who takes their test will be guessing on some of the questions, so they intentionally write wrong answer choices to seem plausible. You still have to pick an answer though, and if the wrong answer choices are designed to look right, how can you ever be sure that you're not falling for their trap? The best solution we've found to this dilemma is to take the decision out of your hands entirely. Here is the process we recommend:

Once you've eliminated any choices that you are confident (willing to bet $5) are wrong, select the first remaining choice as your answer.

Whether you choose to select the first remaining choice, the second, or the last, the important thing is that you use some preselected standard. Using this approach guarantees that you will not be enticed into selecting an answer choice that looks right, because you are not basing your decision on how the answer choices look.

This is not meant to make you question your knowledge. Instead, it is to help you recognize the difference between your knowledge and your impressions. There's a huge difference between thinking an answer is right because of what you know, and thinking an answer is right because it looks or sounds like it should be right.

Summary: To ensure that your selection is appropriately random, make a predetermined selection from among all answer choices you have not eliminated.

Test-Taking Strategies

This section contains a list of test-taking strategies that you may find helpful as you work through the test. By taking what you know and applying logical thought, you can maximize your chances of answering any question correctly!

It is very important to realize that every question is different and every person is different: no single strategy will work on every question, and no single strategy will work for every person. That's why we've included all of them here, so you can try them out and determine which ones work best for different types of questions and which ones work best for you.

Question Strategies

Read Carefully

Read the question and answer choices carefully. Don't miss the question because you misread the terms. You have plenty of time to read each question thoroughly and make sure you understand what is being asked. Yet a happy medium must be attained, so don't waste too much time. You must read carefully, but efficiently.

Contextual Clues

Look for contextual clues. If the question includes a word you are not familiar with, look at the immediate context for some indication of what the word might mean. Contextual clues can often give you all the information you need to decipher the meaning of an unfamiliar word. Even if you can't determine the meaning, you may be able to narrow down the possibilities enough to make a solid guess at the answer to the question.

Prefixes

If you're having trouble with a word in the question or answer choices, try dissecting it. Take advantage of every clue that the word might include. Prefixes and suffixes can be a huge help. Usually they allow you to determine a basic meaning. Pre- means before, post- means after, pro - is positive, de- is negative. From prefixes and suffixes, you can get an idea of the general meaning of the word and try to put it into context.

Hedge Words

Watch out for critical hedge words, such as *likely*, *may*, *can*, *sometimes*, *often*, *almost*, *mostly*, *usually*, *generally*, *rarely*, and *sometimes*. Question writers insert these hedge phrases to cover every possibility. Often an answer choice will be wrong simply because it leaves no room for exception. Be on guard for answer choices that have definitive words such as *exactly* and *always*.

Switchback Words

Stay alert for *switchbacks*. These are the words and phrases frequently used to alert you to shifts in thought. The most common switchback words are *but*, *although*, and *however*. Others include *nevertheless*, *on the other hand*, *even though*, *while*, *in spite of*, *despite*, *regardless of*. Switchback words are important to catch because they can change the direction of the question or an answer choice.

Face Value

When in doubt, use common sense. Accept the situation in the problem at face value. Don't read too much into it. These problems will not require you to make wild assumptions. If you have to go beyond creativity and warp time or space in order to have an answer choice fit the question, then you should move on and consider the other answer choices. These are normal problems rooted in reality. The applicable relationship or explanation may not be readily apparent, but it is there for you to figure out. Use your common sense to interpret anything that isn't clear.

Answer Choice Strategies

Answer Selection

The most thorough way to pick an answer choice is to identify and eliminate wrong answers until only one is left, then confirm it is the correct answer. Sometimes an answer choice may immediately seem right, but be careful. The test writers will usually put more than one reasonable answer choice on each question, so take a second to read all of them and make sure that the other choices are not equally obvious. As long as you have time left, it is better to read every answer choice than to pick the first one that looks right without checking the others.

Answer Choice Families

An answer choice family consists of two (in rare cases, three) answer choices that are very similar in construction and cannot all be true at the same time. If you see two answer choices that are direct opposites or parallels, one of them is usually the correct answer. For instance, if one answer choice says that quantity *x* increases and another either says that quantity *x* decreases (opposite) or says that quantity *y* increases (parallel), then those answer choices would fall into the same family. An answer choice that doesn't match the construction of the answer choice family is more likely to be incorrect. Most questions will not have answer choice families, but when they do appear, you should be prepared to recognize them.

Eliminate Answers

Eliminate answer choices as soon as you realize they are wrong, but make sure you consider all possibilities. If you are eliminating answer choices and realize that the last one you are left with is also wrong, don't panic. Start over and consider each choice again. There may be something you missed the first time that you will realize on the second pass.

Avoid Fact Traps

Don't be distracted by an answer choice that is factually true but doesn't answer the question. You are looking for the choice that answers the question. Stay focused on what the question is asking for so you don't accidentally pick an answer that is true but incorrect. Always go back to the question and make sure the answer choice you've selected actually answers the question and is not merely a true statement.

Extreme Statements

In general, you should avoid answers that put forth extreme actions as standard practice or proclaim controversial ideas as established fact. An answer choice that states the "process should be used in certain situations, if..." is much more likely to be correct than one that states the "process should be discontinued completely." The first is a calm rational statement and doesn't even make a definitive, uncompromising stance, using a hedge word *if* to provide wiggle room, whereas the second choice is a radical idea and far more extreme.

Benchmark

As you read through the answer choices and you come across one that seems to answer the question well, mentally select that answer choice. This is not your final answer, but it's the one that will help you evaluate the other answer choices. The one that you selected is your benchmark or standard for judging each of the other answer choices. Every other answer choice must be compared to your benchmark. That choice is correct until proven otherwise by another answer choice beating it. If you find a better answer, then that one becomes your new benchmark. Once you've decided that no other choice answers the question as well as your benchmark, you have your final answer.

Predict the Answer

Before you even start looking at the answer choices, it is often best to try to predict the answer. When you come up with the answer on your own, it is easier to avoid distractions and traps because you will know exactly what to look for. The right answer choice is unlikely to be word-for-word what you came up with, but it should be a close match. Even if you are confident that you have the right answer, you should still take the time to read each option before moving on.

General Strategies

Tough Questions

If you are stumped on a problem or it appears too hard or too difficult, don't waste time. Move on! Remember though, if you can quickly check for obviously incorrect answer choices, your chances of guessing correctly are greatly improved. Before you completely give up, at least try to knock out a couple of possible answers. Eliminate what you can and then guess at the remaining answer choices before moving on.

Check Your Work

Since you will probably not know every term listed and the answer to every question, it is important that you get credit for the ones that you do know. Don't miss any questions through careless mistakes. If at all possible, try to take a second to look back over your answer selection and make sure you've selected the correct answer choice and haven't made a costly careless mistake (such as marking an answer choice that you didn't mean to mark). This quick double check should more than pay for itself in caught mistakes for the time it costs.

Pace Yourself

It's easy to be overwhelmed when you're looking at a page full of questions; your mind is confused and full of random thoughts, and the clock is ticking down faster than you would like. Calm down and maintain the pace that you have set for yourself. Especially as you get down to the last few minutes of the test, don't let the small numbers on the clock make you panic. As long as you are on track by monitoring your pace, you are guaranteed to have time for each question.

Don't Rush

It is very easy to make errors when you are in a hurry. Maintaining a fast pace in answering questions is pointless if it makes you miss questions that you would have gotten right otherwise. Test writers like to include distracting information and wrong answers that seem right. Taking a little extra time to avoid careless mistakes can make all the difference in your test score. Find a pace that allows you to be confident in the answers that you select.

Keep Moving

Panicking will not help you pass the test, so do your best to stay calm and keep moving. Taking deep breaths and going through the answer elimination steps you practiced can help to break through a stress barrier and keep your pace.

Final Notes

The combination of a solid foundation of content knowledge and the confidence that comes from practicing your plan for applying that knowledge is the key to maximizing your performance on test day. As your foundation of content knowledge is built up and strengthened, you'll find that the strategies included in this chapter become more and more effective in helping you quickly sift through the distractions and traps of the test to isolate the correct answer.

Now it's time to move on to the test content chapters of this book, but be sure to keep your goal in mind. As you read, think about how you will be able to apply this information on the test. If you've already seen sample questions for the test and you have an idea of the question format and style, try to come up with questions of your own that you can answer based on what you're reading. This will give you valuable practice applying your knowledge in the same ways you can expect to on test day.

Good luck and good studying!

Astronomy and Space Science

Astronomy

Astronomy is the scientific study of celestial objects and their positions, movements, and structures. Celestial does not refer to the Earth in particular, but does include its motions as it moves through space. Other objects include the Sun, the Moon, planets, satellites, asteroids, meteors, comets, stars, galaxies, the universe, and other space phenomena. The term astronomy has its roots in the Greek words "astro" and "nomos," which means "laws of the stars."

Universe

What can be seen of the universe is believed to be at least 93 billion light years across. To put this into perspective, the Milky Way galaxy is about 100,000 light years across. Our view of matter in the universe is that it forms into clumps. Matter is organized into stars, galaxies, clusters of galaxies, superclusters, and the Great Wall of galaxies. Galaxies consist of stars, some with planetary systems. Some estimates state that the universe is about 13 billion years old. It is not considered dense, and is believed to consist of 73 percent dark energy, 23 percent cold dark matter, and 4 percent regular matter. Cosmology is the study of the universe. Interstellar medium (ISM) is the gas and dust in the interstellar space between a galaxy's stars.

Origin

The universe can be said to consist of everything and nothing. The universe is the source of everything we know about space, matter, energy, and time. There are likely still phenomena that have yet to be discovered. The universe can also be thought of as nothing, since a vast portion of the known universe is empty space. It is believed that the universe is expanding. The Big Bang theory, which is widely accepted among astronomers, was developed to explain the origin of the universe. There are other theories regarding the origin of the universe, such as the Steady-State theory and the Creationist theory. The Big Bang theory states that all the matter in the universe was once in one place. This matter underwent a huge explosion that spread the matter into space. Galaxies formed from this material and the universe is still expanding.

Galaxies

Galaxies consist of stars, stellar remnants, and dark matter. Dwarf galaxies contain as few as 10 million stars, while giant galaxies contain as many as 1 trillion stars. Galaxies are gravitationally bound, meaning the stars, star systems, other gases, and dust orbits the galaxy's center. The Earth exists in the Milky Way galaxy and the nearest galaxy to ours is the Andromeda galaxy. Galaxies can be classified by their visual shape into elliptical, spiral, irregular, and starburst galaxies. It is estimated that there are more than 100 billion galaxies in the universe ranging from 1,000 to 100,000 parsecs in diameter. Galaxies can be megaparsecs apart. Intergalactic space consists of a gas with an average density of less than one atom per cubic meter. Galaxies are organized into clusters which form superclusters. Dark matter may account for up to 90% of the mass of galaxies. Dark matter is still not well understood.

Solar system

The solar system is a planetary system of objects that exist in an ecliptic plane. Objects orbit around and are bound by gravity to a star called the Sun. Objects that orbit around the Sun include: planets, dwarf planets, moons, asteroids, meteoroids, cosmic dust, and comets. The definition of planets has changed. At one time, there were nine planets in the solar system. There are now eight. Planetary objects in the solar system include four inner, terrestrial planets: Mercury, Venus, Earth, and Mars. They are relatively small, dense, rocky, lack rings, and have few or no moons. The four outer, or Jovian, planets are Jupiter, Saturn, Uranus, and Neptune, which are large and have low densities, rings, and moons. They are also known as gas giants. Between the inner and outer planets is the asteroid belt. Beyond Neptune is the Kuiper belt. Within these belts are five dwarf planets: Ceres, Pluto, Haumea, Makemake, and Eris.

Size

The Earth is about 12,765 km (7,934 miles) in diameter. The Moon is about 3,476 km (2,160 mi) in diameter. The distance between the Earth and the Moon is about 384,401 km (238,910 mi). The diameter of the Sun is approximately 1,390,000 km (866,000 mi). The distance from the Earth to the Sun is 149,598,000 km, also known as 1 Astronomical Unit (AU). The star that is nearest to the solar system is Proxima Centauri. It is about 270,000 AU away. Some distant galaxies are so far away that their light takes several billion years to reach the Earth. In other words, people on Earth see them as they looked billions of years ago.

Formation theories

A planetary system consists of the various non-stellar objects orbiting a star, such as planets, dwarf planets, moons, asteroids, meteoroids, comets, and cosmic dust. The Sun, together with its planetary system, which includes Earth, is known as the solar system. The theory of how the solar system was created is that it started with the collapse of a cloud of interstellar gas and dust, which formed the solar nebula. This collapse is believed to have occurred because the cloud was disturbed. As it collapsed, it heated up and compressed at the center, forming a flatter protoplanetary disk with a protostar at the center. Planets formed as a result of accretion from the disk. Gas cooled and condensed into tiny particles of rock, metal, and ice. These particles collided and formed into larger particles, and then into object the size of small asteroids. Eventually, some became large enough to have significant gravity.

Sun

The Sun is at the center of the solar system. It is composed of 70% hydrogen (H) and 28% helium (He). The remaining 2% is made up of metals. The Sun is one of 100 billion stars in the Milky Way galaxy. Its diameter is 1,390,000 km, its mass is 1.989×10^{30} kg, its surface temperature is 5,800 K, and its core temperature is 15,600,000 K. The Sun represents more than 99.8% of the total mass of the solar system. At the core, the temperature is 15.6 million K, the pressure is 250 billion atmospheres, and the density is more than 150 times that of water. The surface is called the photosphere. The chromosphere lies above this, and the corona, which extends millions of kilometers into space, is next. Sunspots are relatively cool regions on the surface with a temperature of 3,800 K. Temperatures in the corona are over 1,000,000 K. Its magnetosphere, or heliosphere, extends far beyond Pluto.

Energy

The Sun's energy is produced by nuclear fusion reactions. Each second, about 700,000,000 tons of hydrogen are converted (or fused) to about 695,000,000 tons of helium and 5,000,000 tons of energy in the form of gamma rays. In nuclear fusion, four hydrogen nuclei are fused into one helium nucleus, resulting in the release of energy. In the Sun, the energy proceeds towards the surface and is absorbed and re-emitted at lower and lower temperatures. Energy is mostly in the form of visible light when it reaches the surface. It is estimated that the Sun has used up about half of the hydrogen at its core since its birth. It is expected to radiate in this fashion for another 5 billion years.

Eventually, it will deplete its hydrogen fuel, grow brighter, expand to about 260 times its diameter, and become a red giant. The outer layers will ablate and become a dense white dwarf the size of the Earth.

Inner terrestrial planets

The four inner terrestrial planets are:

- Mercury: Mercury is the closest to the Sun and is also the smallest planet. It orbits the Sun every 88 days, has no satellites or atmosphere, has a Moon-like surface with craters, appears bright, and is dense and rocky with a large iron core.
- Venus: Venus is the second planet from the Sun. It orbits the Sun every 225 days, is very bright, and is similar to Earth in size, gravity, and bulk composition. It has a dense atmosphere composed of carbon dioxide and some sulfur. It is covered with reflective clouds made of sulfuric acid and exhibits signs of volcanism. Lightning and thunder have been recorded on Venus's surface.
- Earth: Earth is the third planet from the Sun. It orbits the Sun every 365 days. Approximately 71% of its surface is salt-water oceans. The Earth is rocky, has an atmosphere composed mainly of oxygen and nitrogen, has one moon, and supports millions of species. It contains the only known life in the solar system.
- Mars: Mars it the fourth planet from the Sun. It appears reddish due to iron oxide on the surface, has a thin atmosphere, has a rotational period similar to Earth's, and has seasonal cycles. Surface features of Mars include volcanoes, valleys, deserts, and polar ice caps. Mars has impact craters and the tallest mountain, largest canyon, and perhaps the largest impact crater yet discovered.

Gas giant planets

The four outer, gas giant planets are:

- Jupiter: Jupiter is the fifth planet from the Sun and the largest planet in the solar system. It consists mainly of hydrogen, and 25% of its mass is made up of helium. It has a fast rotation and has clouds in the tropopause composed of ammonia crystals that are arranged into bands sub-divided into lighter-hued zones and darker belts causing storms and turbulence. Jupiter has wind speeds of 100 m/s, a planetary ring, 63 moons, and a Great Red Spot, which is an anticyclonic storm.
- Saturn: Saturn is the sixth planet from the Sun and the second largest planet in the solar system. It is composed of hydrogen, some helium, and trace elements. Saturn has a small core of rock and ice, a thick layer of metallic hydrogen, a gaseous outer layer, wind speeds of up to 1,800 km/h, a system of rings, and 61 moons.
- Uranus: Uranus is the seventh planet from the Sun. Its atmosphere is composed mainly of hydrogen and helium, and also contains water, ammonia, methane, and traces of hydrocarbons. With a minimum temperature of 49 K, Uranus has the coldest atmosphere. Uranus has a ring system, a magnetosphere, and 13 moons.
- Neptune: Neptune is the eighth planet from the Sun and is the planet with the third largest mass. It has 12 moons, an atmosphere similar to Uranus, a Great Dark Spot, and the strongest sustained winds of any planet (wind speeds can be as high as 2,100 km/h). Neptune is cold (about 55 K) and has a fragmented ring system.

Phases of the Moon

It takes about one month for the Moon to go through all its phases. Waxing refers to the two weeks during which the Moon goes from a new moon to a full moon. About two weeks is spent waning, going from a full moon to a new moon. The lit part of the Moon always faces the Sun. The phases of waxing are: new moon, during which the Moon is not illuminated and rises and sets with the Sun; crescent moon, during which a tiny sliver is lit; first quarter, during which half the Moon is lit and the phase of the Moon is due south on the meridian; gibbous, during which more than half of the Moon is lit and has a shape similar to a football; right side, during which the Moon is lit; and full moon, during which the Moon is fully illuminated, rises at sunset, and sets at sunrise. After a full moon, the Moon is waning. The phases of waning are: gibbous, during which the left side is lit and the Moon rises after sunset and sets after sunrise; third quarter, during which the Moon is half lit and rises at midnight and sets at noon; crescent, during which a tiny sliver is lit; and new moon, during which the Moon is not illuminated and rises and sets with the Sun.

Stars

Birth

A nebula is a cloud of dust and gas that is composed primarily of hydrogen (97%) and helium (3%). Gravity causes parts of the nebula to clump together. This accretion continues adding atoms to the center of an unstable protostar. Equilibrium between gravity pulling atoms and gas pressure pushing heat and light away from the center is achieved. A star dies when it is no longer able to maintain equilibrium. A protostar may never become a star if it does not reach a critical core temperature. It may become a brown dwarf or a gas giant instead. If nuclear fusion of hydrogen into helium begins, a star is born. The "main sequence" of a star's life involves nuclear fusion reactions. During this time, the star contracts over billions of years to compensate for the heat and light energy lost. In the star's core, temperature, density, and pressure increase as the star contracts and the cycle continues.

Life cycle

There are different life cycle possibilities for stars after they initially form and enter into the main sequence stage. Small, relatively cold red dwarfs with relatively low masses burn hydrogen slowly, and will remain in the main sequence for hundreds of billions of years. Massive, hot supergiants will leave the main sequence after just a few million years. The Sun is a mid-sized star that may be in the main sequence for 10 billion years. After the main sequence, the star expands to become a red giant. Depending upon the initial mass of the star, it can become a black dwarf (from a medium-sized star), and then a small, cooling white dwarf. Massive stars become red supergiants (and sometimes blue supergiants), explode in a supernova, and then become neutron stars. The largest stars can become black holes.

Astronomical unit, light year, and parsec

An astronomical unit, also known as AU, is a widely used measurement in astronomy. One AU is equal to the distance from the Earth to the Sun, which is 150 million km, or 93 million miles. These distances can also be expressed as 149.60×10^9 m or 92.956×10^6 mi. A light year (ly) is the distance that light travels in a vacuum in one year. A light year is equal to about 10 trillion km, or 64,341 AU, and is used to measure large astronomical units. Also used for measuring large distances is the parsec (pc), which is the preferred unit since it is better suited for recording observational data. A parsec is the parallax of one arcsecond, and is about 31 trillion km (about 19 trillion miles), or about 3.26 light years. It is used to calculate distances by triangulation. The AU distance from the Earth to the Sun is used to form the side of a right triangle.

Sidereal days and solar days

A sidereal day is four minutes shorter than a solar day. A solar day is the time it takes the Earth to complete one revolution and face the Sun again. From noon to noon is 24 hours. A sidereal day is measured against a distant "fixed" star. As the Earth completes one rotation, it has also completed part of its revolution around the Sun, so it completes a sidereal rotation in reference to the fixed star before it completes a solar rotation. The Sun travels along the ecliptic in 365.25 days. This can be tracked day after day before dawn. After one year, the stars appear back in their original positions. As a result, different constellations are viewable at different times of the year. Sidereal years are slightly longer than tropical years. The difference is caused by the precession of the equinoxes. A calendar based on the sidereal year will be out of sync with the seasons at a rate of about one day every 71 years.

Oort Cloud, the asteroid belt, and the Kuiper Belt

The asteroid belt is between Mars and Jupiter. The many objects contained within are composed of rock and metal similar to those found on the terrestrial planets. The Kuiper Belt is beyond Neptune's orbit, but the influence of the gas giants may cause objects from the Kuiper Belt to cross Neptune's orbit. Objects in the Kuiper Belt are still being discovered. They are thought to be composed of the frozen forms of water, ammonia, and methane, and may be the source of short-period comets. It is estimated that there are 35,000 Kuiper Belt objects greater than 100 km in diameter and perhaps 100 million objects about 20 km in diameter. There is also a hypothetical Oort Cloud that may exist far beyond the Kuiper Belt and act as a source for long-period comets.

Comets

A comet consists of frozen gases and rocky and metallic materials. Comets are usually small and typically have long tails. A comet's tail is made of ionized gases. It points away from the Sun and follows the comet as it approaches the Sun. The tail precedes the head as the comet moves away from the Sun. It is believed that as many as 100 billion comets exist. About 12 new ones are discovered each year. Their orbits are elliptical, not round. Some scientists theorize that short-period comets originate from the Kuiper Belt and long-period comets originate from the Oort Cloud, which is thought to be 100,000 AU away. Comets orbit the Sun in time periods varying from a few years to hundreds of thousands of years. A well-known comet, Halley's Comet, has an orbit of 76 years. It is 80 percent water, and consists of frozen water, carbon dioxide (dry ice), ammonia, and methane.

Meteors, meteoroids, and meteorites

A meteoroid is the name for a rock from space before it enters the Earth's atmosphere. Most meteoroids burn up in the atmosphere before reaching altitudes of 80 km. A meteor is the streak of light from a meteoroid in the Earth's atmosphere, and is also known as a shooting star. Meteor showers are associated with comets, happen when the Earth passes through the debris of a comet, and are associated with a higher than normal number of meteors. Meteorites are rocks that reach the Earth's surface from space. Fireballs are very bright meteors with trails that can last as long as 30 minutes. A bolide is a fireball that burns up when it enters Earth's atmosphere. There are many types of meteorites, and they are known to be composed of various materials. Iron meteorites consist of iron and nickel with a criss-cross, or Widmanstatten, internal metallic crystalline structure. Stony iron meteorites are composed of iron, nickel, and silicate materials. Stony meteorites consist mainly of silicate and also contain iron and nickel.

Natural satellites

There are about 335 moons, or satellites, that orbit the planets and objects in the solar system. Many of these satellites have been recently discovered, a few are theoretical, some are asteroid moons (moons orbiting asteroids), some are moonlets (small moons), and some are moons of dwarf planets and objects that have not been definitively categorized, such as trans-Neptunian objects. Mercury and Venus do not have any moons. There are several moons larger than the dwarf planet Pluto and two larger than Mercury. Some consider the Earth and Moon a pair of double planets rather than a planet and a satellite. Some satellites may have started out as asteroids. They were eventually captured by a planet's gravity and became moons.

Geometry of the Earth-Moon-Sun system

The Earth-Moon-Sun system is responsible for eclipses. From Earth, the Sun and the Moon appear to be about the same size. An eclipse of the Sun occurs during a new Moon, when the side of the Moon facing the Earth is not illuminated. The Moon passes in front of the Sun and blocks its view from Earth. Eclipses do not occur every month because the orbit of the Moon is at about a 5° angle to the plane of Earth's orbit. An eclipse of the Moon happens during the full Moon phase. The Moon passes through the shadow of the Earth and blocks sunlight from reaching it, which temporarily causes darkness. During a lunar eclipse, there are two parts to the shadow. The umbra is the dark, inner region. The sun is completely blocked in this area. The penumbra is a partially lighted area around the umbra. Earth's shadow is four times longer than the Moon's shadow.

Remote sensing

Remote sensing refers to the gathering of data about an object or phenomenon without physical or intimate contact with the object being studied. The data can be viewed or recorded and stored in many forms (visually with a camera, audibly, or in the form of data). Gathering weather data from a ship, satellite, or buoy might be thought of as remote sensing. The monitoring of a fetus through the use of ultrasound technology provides a remote image. Listening to the heartbeat of a fetus is another example of remote sensing. Methods for remote sensing can be grouped as radiometric, geodetic, or acoustic. Examples of radiometric remote sensing include radar, laser altimeters, light detection and ranging (LIDAR) used to determine the concentration of chemicals in the air, and radiometers used to detect various frequencies of radiation. Geodetic remote sensing involves measuring the small fluctuations in Earth's gravitational field. Examples of acoustic remote sensing include underwater sonar and seismographs.

Geosynchronous and geostationary orbits

A geosynchronous orbit around the Earth has an orbital period matching the Earth's sidereal rotation period. Sidereal rotation is based on the position of a fixed star, not the Sun, so a sidereal day is slightly shorter than a 24-hour solar day. A satellite in a geosynchronous orbit appears in the same place in the sky at the same time each day. Technically, any object with an orbit time period equal to the Earth's rotational period is geosynchronous. A geostationary orbit is a geosynchronous orbit that is circular and at zero inclination, which means the object is located directly above the equator. Geostationary orbits are useful for communications satellites because they are fixed in the same spot relative to the Earth. A semisynchronous orbit has an orbital period of half a sidereal day.

Notable satellites

The first satellite to orbit the Earth was the Soviet Union's Sputnik 1 in 1957. Its two radio transmitters emitted beeps that were received by radios around the world. Analysis of the radio signals was used to gather information about the electron density of the ionosphere. Soviet success escalated the American space program. In 1958, the U.S. put Explorer 1 into orbit. The Osumi was the first Japanese satellite, which was put into orbit in 1970. The Vanguard 1 is the satellite that has orbited the Earth the longest. It was put into orbit in 1958 and was still in orbit in June, 2009. The Mir Space Station orbited Earth for 11 years, and was assembled in space starting in 1986. It was almost continuously occupied until 1999. The International Space Station began being assembled in orbit in 1998. At 43,000 cubic feet, it is the largest manned object sent into space. It circles the Earth every 90 minutes.

Piloted space missions

The Soviet space program successfully completed the first space flight by orbiting Yuri Gagarin in 1961 on Vostok 1. His orbit lasted 1 hour, 48 minutes. Later in 1961, the U.S. completed its first piloted space flight by launching Alan Shepard into space in the Mercury-Redstone 3. This space mission was suborbital. The first woman in space was Valentina Tereshkova, who orbited the Earth 48 times aboard Vostok 6 in 1963. The first space flight with more than one person and also the first that didn't involve space suits took place on the Voskhod in 1964. The first person on the Moon was American Neil Armstrong. In 1969, he traveled to the Moon on Apollo 11, which was the 11th manned space flight completed in the Apollo program, which was conducted from 1968 to 1972. In 2003, Yang Liwei became the first person from China to go into space. He traveled onboard the Shenzhou 5. The Space Shuttle Orbiter has included piloted space shuttles from 1981 until the present. The program was suspended after two space shuttle disasters: Challenger in 1986 and Columbia in 2003.

Unpiloted space missions

The first artificial object to reach another space object was Luna 2. It crashed on the Moon in 1959. The first automatic landing was by Luna 9. It landed on the Moon in 1966. Mariner 2's flyby of Venus in 1962 was the first successful interplanetary flyby. Venera 7 landing on and transmitting data from Venus was the first interplanetary surface landing, which took place in 1970. The first soft landing on Mars was in 1971. Unpiloted spacecraft have also made successful soft landings on the asteroids Eros and Itokawa, as well as Titan, a moon of Saturn. The first flyby of Jupiter was in 1973 by Pioneer 10. Pioneer 10 was also the first craft of its kind to leave the solar system. The first flyby of Mercury was in 1974 by Mariner. The first flyby of Saturn was in 1979 by Pioneer 11. The first flyby of Uranus was in 1986 by Voyager 2, which also flew by Neptune in 1989.

Limitations of space exploration

There are many limitations of space exploration. The main limitation is knowledge. Space exploration is currently time-consuming, dangerous, and costly. Manned and unmanned missions, even within the solar system, take years of planning and years to complete. The associated financial costs are great. Interstellar travel and intergalactic is not yet realistically feasible. Technological advances are needed before these types of missions can be carried out. By some estimates, it would take more than 70 years to travel to Proxima Centauri (the nearest star) using the fastest rocket technology available. It would take much longer using less advanced technologies. Space travel is dangerous for many reasons. Rocket fuel is highly explosive. Non-Earth environments are uninhabitable for humans. Finally, astronauts are exposed to larger than usual amounts of radiation.

Geology

Rocks and minerals

Minerals are naturally occurring, inorganic solids with a definite chemical composition and an orderly internal crystal structure. A polymorph is two minerals with the same chemical composition, but a different crystal structure. Rocks are aggregates of one or more minerals, and may also contain mineraloids (minerals lacking a crystalline structure) and organic remains. The three types of rocks are sedimentary, igneous, and metamorphic. Rocks are classified based on their formation and the minerals they contain. Minerals are classified by their chemical composition. Geology is the study of the planet Earth as it pertains to the composition, structure, and origin of its rocks. Petrology is the study of rocks, including their composition, texture, structure, occurrence, mode of formation, and history. Mineralogy is the study of minerals.

Identification

The physical properties (as opposed to chemical structures) used to identify minerals are hardness, luster, color, cleavage, streak, form (the external shape), and other special properties. Senses other than sight, such as touch, taste, and smell, may be used to observe physical properties. Hardness is the resistance a mineral has to scratches. The Mohs Hardness Scale is used to rate hardness from 1 to 10. Color can often not be determined definitively as some minerals can be more than one color. Luster is determined by reflected light. Luster can be described as metallic (shiny), sub-metallic (dull), non-metallic (vitreous, like glass), or earthy (like dirt or powder). Streak is the true color of the mineral in powdered form. It can be determined by rubbing the specimen across an unglazed porcelain tile. Fracture or cleavage is how a mineral reacts to stress, such as being struck with a hammer. Other properties that can be used to identify rocks and minerals include magnetism, a salty taste, or a pungent odor in a streak test.

Classification of minerals

Minerals are classified by chemical composition and internal crystalline structure. They are organized into classes. Native elements such as gold and silver are not classified in this manner. The eight classes are sulfides, oxides\hydroxides, halides, carbonates, sulfates, phosphates, and silicates. These classes are based on the dominant anion (negatively charged ion) or anionic group. Minerals are classified in this way for three main reasons. First, minerals with the same anion have unmistakable resemblances. Second, minerals with the same anion are often found in the same geologic environment. For example, calcite and dolomite, which belong to the same group, are often found together. Last, this method is similar to the naming convention used to identify inorganic compounds in chemistry. Minerals can be further separated into groups on the basis of internal structure.

Sedimentary rock

Sedimentary rocks are formed by the process of lithification, which involves compaction, the expulsion of liquids from pores, and the cementation of the pre-existing rock. It is pressure and temperature that are responsible for this process. Sedimentary rocks are often formed in layers in the presence of water, and may contain organic remains, such as fossils. Sedimentary rocks are organized into three groups: detrital, biogenic, and chemical. Texture refers to the size, shape, and grains of sedimentary rock. Texture can be used to determine how a particular sedimentary rock was created. Composition refers to the types of minerals present in the rock. The origin of sedimentary rock refers to the type of water that was involved in its creation. Marine deposits, for example, likely involved ocean environments, while continental deposits likely involved dry land and lakes.

Igneous rock

Igneous rock is formed from magma, which is molten material originating from beneath the Earth's surface. Depending upon where magma cools, the resulting igneous rock can be classified as intrusive, plutonic, hypabyssal, extrusive, or volcanic. Magma that solidifies at a depth is intrusive, cools slowly, and has a coarse grain as a result. An example is granite. Magma that solidifies at or near the surface is extrusive, cools quickly, and usually has a fine grain. An example is basalt. Magma that actually flows out of the Earth's surface is called lava. Some extrusive rock cools so quickly that crystals do not have time to form. These rocks have a glassy appearance. An example is obsidian. Hypabyssal rock is igneous rock that is formed at medium depths.

Metamorphic rock

Metamorphic rock is that which has been changed by great heat and pressure. This results in a variety of outcomes, including deformation, compaction, destruction of the characteristics of the original rock, bending, folding, and formation of new minerals because of chemical reactions, and changes in the size and shape of the mineral grain. For example, the igneous rock ferromagnesian can be changed into schist and gneiss. The sedimentary rock carbonaceous can be changed into marble. The texture of metamorphic rocks can be classified as foliated and unfoliated. Foliation, or layering, occurs when rock is compressed along one axis during recrystallization. This can be seen in schist and shale. Unfoliated rock does not include this banding. Rocks that are compressed equally from all sides or lack specific minerals will be unfoliated. An example is marble.

Earth's structure

The Earth is ellipsoid, not perfectly spherical. This means the diameter is different through the poles and at the equator. Through the poles, the Earth is about 12,715 km in diameter. The approximate center of the Earth is at a depth of 6,378 km. The Earth is divided into a crust, mantle, and core. The core consists of a solid inner portion. Moving outward, the molten outer core occupies the space from about a depth of 5,150 km to a depth of 2,890 km. The mantle consists of a lower and upper layer. The lower layer includes the D' (D prime) and D" (D double-prime) layers. The solid portion of the upper mantle and crust together form the lithosphere, or rocky sphere. Below this, but still within the mantle, is the asthenosphere, or weak sphere. These layers are distinguishable because the lithosphere is relatively rigid, while the asthenosphere resembles a thick liquid.

Plate tectonic theory

The theory of plate tectonics states that the lithosphere, the solid portion of the mantle and Earth's crust, consists of major and minor plates. These plates are on top of and move with the viscous upper mantle, which is heated because of the convection cycle that occurs in the interior of the Earth. There are different estimates as to the exact number of major and minor plates. The number of major plates is believed to be between 9 and 15, and it is thought that there may be as many as 40 minor plates. The United States is atop the North American plate. The Pacific Ocean is atop the Pacific plate. The point at which these two plates slide horizontally along the San Andreas Fault is an example of a transform plate boundary. The other two types of boundaries are divergent (plates that are spreading apart and forming new crust) and convergent (the process of subduction causes one plate to go under another). The movement of plates is what causes other features of the Earth's crust, such as mountains, volcanoes, and earthquakes.

Volcanic activities and plate tectonics

Volcanoes can occur along any type of tectonic plate boundary. At a divergent boundary, as plates move apart, magma rises to the surface, cools, and forms a ridge. An example of this is the mid-Atlantic ridge. Convergent boundaries, where one plate slides under another, are often areas with a lot of volcanic activity. The subduction process creates magma. When it rises to the surface, volcanoes can be created. Volcanoes can also be created in the middle of a plate over hot spots. Hot spots are locations where narrow plumes of magma rise through the mantle in a fixed place over a long period of time. The Hawaiian Islands and Midway are examples. The plate shifts and the island moves. Magma continues to rise through the mantle, however, which produces another island. Volcanoes can be active, dormant, or extinct. Active volcanoes are those that are erupting or about to erupt. Dormant volcanoes are those that might erupt in the future and still have internal volcanic activity. Extinct volcanoes are those that will not erupt.

The three types of volcanoes are shield, cinder cone, and composite. A shield volcano is created by a long-term, relatively gentle eruption. This type of volcanic mountain is created by each progressive lava flow that occurs over time. A cinder cone volcano is created by explosive eruptions. Lava is spewed out of a vent into the air. As it falls to the ground, the lava cools into cinders and ash, which build up around the volcano in a cone shape. A composite volcano is a combination of the other two types of volcanoes. In this type, there are layers of lava flows and layers of ash and cinder.

Earth's chemical composition

The Earth's core consists of hot iron and forms of nickel. The mantle consists of different materials, including iron, magnesium, and calcium. The crust covers the mantle, consists of a thin layer of much lighter rocks, and is further subdivided into continental and oceanic portions. The continental portion consists mainly of silicates, such as granite. The oceanic portion consists of heavier, volcanic rocks, such as basalt. The upper 10 miles of the lithosphere layer (the crust and part of the mantle) is made up of 95% igneous rock (or its metamorphic equivalent), 4% shale, 0.75% sandstone, and 0.25% limestone. There are over 4,000 known minerals, but only about 20 make up some 95% of all rocks. There are, however, more than 3,000 individual kinds of minerals in the Earth's crust. Silicates are the largest group of minerals.

Orogeny

Orogeny refers to the formation of mountains, particularly the processes of folding and faulting caused by plate tectonics. Folding is when layers of sedimentary rock are pressed together by continental plate movements. Sections of rock that are folded upward are called anticlines. Sections of rock that are folded downward are called synclines. Examples of folded mountains are the Alps and the Himalayans. Fault-block mountains are created when tectonic plate movement produces tension that results in displacement. Mountains in the Southwest United States are examples of fault-blocking mountains. Mountains can also be caused by volcanic activity and erosion.

Earthquakes

Most earthquakes are caused by tectonic plate movement. They occur along fractures called faults or fault zones. Friction in the faults prevents smooth movement. Tension builds up over time, and the release of that tension results in earthquakes. Faults are grouped based on the type of slippage that occurs. The types of faults are dip-slip, strike-slip, and oblique-slip. A dip-slip fault involves vertical movement along the fault plane. In a normal dip-slip fault, the wall that is above the fault plane moves down. In a reverse dip-slip fault, the wall above the fault plane moves up. A strike-slip fault involves horizontal movement along the fault plane. Oblique-slip faults involve both vertical and horizontal movement. The Richter magnitude scale measures how much seismic energy was released by an earthquake.

Erosion

Erosion is the wearing away of rock materials from the Earth's surface. Erosion can be classified as natural geologic erosion and erosion due to human activity. Natural geologic erosion occurs due to weathering and gravity. Factors involved in natural geologic erosion are typically long term forces. Human activity such as development, farming, and deforestation occurs over shorter periods of time. Soil, which supports plant growth, is the topmost layer of organic material. One type of erosion is sheet erosion, which is the gradual and somewhat uniform removal of surface soil. Rills are small rivulets that cut into soil. Gullies are rills that have become enlarged due to extended water run-off. Sandblows are caused by wind blowing away particles. Negative effects of erosion include sedimentation in rivers, which can pollute water and damage ecosystems. Erosion can also result in the removal of topsoil, which destroys crops and prevents plants from growing. This reduces food production and alters ecosystems.

Mechanical and chemical weathering

There are two basic types of weathering: mechanical and chemical. Weathering is a very prominent process on the Earth's surface. Materials weather at different rates, which are known as differential weathering. Mechanical and chemical weathering is interdependent. For example, chemical weathering can loosen the bonds between molecules and allow mechanical weathering to take place. Mechanical weathering can expose the surfaces of land masses and allow chemical weathering to take place. Impact, abrasion, frost wedging, root wedging, salt wedging, and uploading are types of mechanical weathering. Types of chemical weathering are dissolution, hydration, hydrolysis, oxidation, biological, and carbonation. The primary type of chemical weathering is caused by water dissolving a mineral. The more acidic water is, the more effective it is at weathering. Carbonic and sulfuric acids can enter rain when they are present in the atmosphere. This lowers the pH value of rain, making it more acidic. Normal rain water has a pH value of 5.5. Acid rain has a pH value of 4 or less.

Deposition

Deposition, or sedimentation, is the geological process in which previously eroded material is transported or added to a land form or land mass. Erosion and sedimentation are complementary geological processes. Running water causes a substantial amount of deposition of transported materials in both fresh water and coastal areas. Examples include gravity transporting material down the slope of a mountain and depositing it at the base of the slope. Another example is when sandstorms deposit particles in other locations. When glaciers melt and retreat, it can result in the deposition of sediments. Evaporation is also considered to cause deposition since dissolved materials are left behind when water evaporates. Deposition can include the buildup of organic materials. For example, chalk is partially made up of the small calcium carbonate skeletons of marine plankton, which helps create more calcium carbonate from chemical processes.

Uniformitarianism, catastrophism, and superposition

Also known as gradualism, uniformitarianism is the belief among modern geologists that the forces, processes, and laws that we see today have existed throughout geologic time. It involves the belief that the present is the key to the past, and that relatively slow processes have shaped the geological features of Earth. Catastrophism is the belief that the Earth was shaped by sudden, short-term catastrophic events. In geology, and in the field of stratigraphy in particular, the law of superposition is that underground layers closer to the surface were deposited more recently.

Stratigraphy and subfields

Stratigraphy is a branch of geology that involves the study of rock layers and layering. Sedimentary rocks are the primary focus of stratigraphy. Subfields include lithostratigraphy, which is the study of the vertical layering of rock types, and biostratigraphy, which is the study of fossil evidence in rock layers. Magnetostratigraphy is the study of changes in detrital remnant magnetism (DRM), which is used to measure the polarity of Earth's magnetic field at the time a stratum was deposited. Chronostratigraphy focuses on the relative dating of rock strata based on the time of rock formation. Unconformity refers to missing layers of rock.

Relative and absolute time

A numerical, or "absolute," age is a specific number of years, such as 150 million years ago. A "relative" age refers to a time range, such as the Mesozoic era. It is used to determine whether one rock formation is older or younger than another formation. Radioactive dating is a form of absolute dating and stratigraphy is a form of relative dating. Radioactive dating techniques have provided the most information about the absolute age of rocks and other geological features. Together, geochronologists have created a geologic time scale. Biostratigraphy uses plant and animal fossils within rock to determine its relative age.

Fossils

Fossils are preservations of plants, animals, their remains, or their traces that date back to about 10,000 years ago. Fossils and where they are found in rock strata makes up the fossil record. Fossils are formed under a very specific set of conditions. The fossil must not be damaged by predators and scavengers after death, and the fossil must not decompose. Usually, this happens when the organism is quickly covered with sediment. This sediment builds up and molecules in the organism's body are replaced by minerals. Fossils come in an array of sizes, from single-celled organisms to large dinosaurs.

Fossils provide a wealth of information about the past, particularly about the flora and fauna that once occupied the Earth, but also about the geologic history of the Earth itself and how Earth and its inhabitants came to be. Some fossilized remains in the geohistorical record exemplify ongoing processes in the Earth's environment, such as weathering, glaciation, and volcanism. These have all led to evolutionary changes in plants and animals. Other fossils support the theory that catastrophic events caused drastic changes in the Earth and its living creatures. One example of this type of theory is that a meteor struck the Earth and caused dinosaurs to become extinct. Both types of fossils provide scientists with a way to hypothesize whether these types of events will happen again.

Geologic time scale

Geologists use the geologic time scale when discussing Earth's chronology and the formation of rocks and minerals. Age is calculated in millions of years before the present time. Units of time are often delineated by geologic or paleontologic events. Smaller units of time such as eras are distinguished by the abundance and/or extinction of certain plant and animal life. For example, the extinction of the dinosaurs marks the end of the Mesozoic era and the beginning of the Cenozoic, the present, era. We are in the Holocene epoch. The supereon encompasses the greatest amount of time. It is composed of eons. Eons are divided into eras, eras into periods, and periods into epochs.

Layers of rock also correspond to periods of time in geochronology. Current theory holds that the Earth was formed 4.5 billion years ago.

Development of geologic time scale

The first known observations of stratigraphy were made by Aristotle, who lived before the time of Christ. He observed seashells in ancient rock formations and on the beach, and concluded that the fossilized seashells were similar to current seashells. Avicenna, a Persian scholar from the 11th century, also made early advances in the development of stratigraphy with the concept of superposition. Nicolas Steno, a Danish scientist from the 17th century, expounded upon this with the belief that layers of rock are piled on top of each other. In the 18th century, Abraham Werner categorized rocks from four different periods: the Primary, Secondary, Tertiary, and Quaternary periods. This fell out of use when the belief emerged that rock layers containing the same fossils had been deposited at the same time, and were therefore from the same age. British geologists created the names for many of the time divisions in use today. For example, the Devonian period was named after the county of Devon, and the Permian period was named after Perm, Russia.

Formation of the Earth

Earth's early development began after a supernova exploded. This led to the formation of the Sun out of hydrogen gas and interstellar dust. These same elements swirled around the newly-formed Sun and formed the planets, including Earth. Scientists theorize that about 4.5 billion years ago, Earth was a chunk of rock surrounded by a cloud of gas. It is believed it lacked water and the type of atmosphere that exists today. Heat from radioactive materials in the rock and pressure in the Earth's interior melted the interior. This caused the heavier materials, such as iron, to sink. Lighter silicate-type rocks rose to the Earth's surface. These rocks formed the Earth's earliest crust. Other chemicals also rose to the Earth's surface, helping to form the water and atmosphere. There is one material that has been dated by scientists and found to be 4.4 billion years old. The material is zircon, which consists of zirconium, silicon, and oxygen. Zircon is a mineral that has a high resistance to weathering.

Paleozoic era

The Paleozoic era began about 542 Ma and lasted until 251 Ma. It is further divided into six periods. The Paleozoic era began after the supercontinent Pannotia started to break up and at the end of a global ice age. By the end of the era, the supercontinent Pangaea had formed. The beginning of the Paleozoic era is marked by Cambrian Explosion, a time when there were abundant life forms according to the fossil record. The end of the era is marked by one of the major extinction events, the Permian extinction, during which almost 90 percent of the species living at the time became extinct. Many plant and animal forms appeared on the land and in the sea during this era. It is also when large land plants first appeared in the fossil record. There are many invertebrates found in the fossil record of the Paleozoic era, and fish, amphibians, and reptiles also first appeared in the fossil record during this era. There were also large swamps and forests, some of which were formed into coal deposits that exist today.

Mesozoic era

The Mesozoic era is known as the Age of the Dinosaurs. It is also the era during which the dinosaurs became extinct. The fossil record also shows the appearance of mammals and birds. Trees that existed included gymnosperms, which have uncovered seeds and are mostly cone bearing, and angiosperms, which have covered seeds and are flowering plants. The angiosperm group is currently the dominant plant group. It was also during this era that the supercontinent Pangaea divided into the continental pieces that exist today. During the Cretaceous period, sea levels rose until one-third of the Earth's present land mass was underwater, and then receded. This period created huge marine deposits and chalk. The extinction of the dinosaurs happened about 65 Ma, and was believed to have been triggered by the impact of an asteroid.

Cenozoic era

The Cenozoic era began about 65.5 Ma and continues to the present. It is marked by the Cretaceous-Tertiary extinction event (extinction of the dinosaurs as well as many invertebrates and plants). The Cenozoic era is further divided into the Paleogene, Neogene, and Quaternary periods. During the Cenozoic era, Pangaea continued to drift, and the plates eventually moved into their present positions. The Pleistocene Ice Age, also known as Quaternary glaciation or the current ice age began about 2.58 Ma and includes the glaciation occurring today. Mammals continued to evolve and other plants and animals came into existence during this era. The fossil record includes the ancestors of the horse, rhinoceros, and camel. It also includes the first dogs and cats and the first humanlike creatures. The first humans appeared less than 200,000 years ago.

Meteorology, Oceanography, and Groundwater

The Ocean

The ocean is the salty body of water that encompasses the Earth. It has a mass of 1.4×10^{24} grams. Geographically, the ocean is divided into three large oceans: the Pacific Ocean, the Atlantic Ocean, and the Indian Ocean. There are also other divisions, such as gulfs, bays, and various types of seas, including Mediterranean and marginal seas. Ocean distances can be measured by latitude, longitude, degrees, meters, miles, and nautical miles. The ocean accounts for 70.8% of the surface of the Earth, amounting to 361,254,000 km^2. The ocean's depth is greatest at Challenger Deep in the Mariana Trench. The ocean floor here is 10,924 meters below sea level. The depths of the ocean are mapped by echo sounders and satellite altimeter systems. Echo sounders emit a sound pulse from the surface and record the time it takes to return. Satellite altimeters provide better maps of the ocean floor.

Ocean floor

The ocean floor includes features similar to those found on land, such as mountains, ridges, plains, and canyons. The oceanic crust is a thin, dense layer that is about 10 km thick. The greatest volume of water is contained in the basins with lesser volumes that occupy the low-lying areas of the continents, which are known as the continental shelves. The continental slope connects the shelf to the ocean floor of the basin. The continental rise is a slightly sloping area between the slope and the basin. A seamount is an undersea volcanic peak that rises to a height of at least 1,000 meters. A guyot is a seamount with a flat top. A mid-ocean ridge is a continuous undersea mountain chain. Sills are low parts of ridges separating ocean basins or other seas. Trenches are long, narrow troughs. Many isolated peaks and seamounts are scattered throughout the ocean basins, and interrupt ocean currents.

Ocean currents

Surface currents are caused by winds. Subsurface currents, which occur deep beneath the ocean's surface, are caused by land masses and the Earth's rotation. The density of ocean water can also affect currents. Sea water with a higher salinity is denser than sea water with a lower salinity. Water from denser areas flows to areas with water that is less dense. Currents are classified by temperature. Colder polar sea water flows south towards warmer water, forming cold currents. Warm water currents swirl around the basins and equator. In turn, heat lost and gained by the ocean creates winds. Ocean currents play a significant role in transferring this heat toward the poles, which aids in the development of many types of weather phenomena.

Gyres and the Coriolis effect

Gyres are surface ocean currents that form large circular patterns. In the Northern Hemisphere, they flow clockwise. In the Southern Hemisphere, they flow counterclockwise. These directions are caused by the Coriolis effect. The Coriolis effect occurs due to the fact that the Earth is a rotating object. In the Northern Hemisphere, currents appear to be curving to the right. In the Southern Hemisphere, currents appear to be curving to the left. This is because the Earth is rotating. Gyres tend to flow in the opposite direction near the Earth's poles. In the portion of the Pacific Ocean north of the equator, the major currents are North Pacific, California, North Equatorial, and Kuroshio. In the South Pacific, they are South Equatorial, East Australia, South Pacific, and Peru. In the North Atlantic, they are the North Atlantic Drift, Canary, North Equatorial, and Gulf Stream. In the South Atlantic, they are South Equatorial, Brazil, South Atlantic, and Benguela.

Ocean waves

Most waves in the ocean are formed by winds. The stronger the winds are, the larger the waves will be. The highest point of a wave is the crest. The lowest point of a wave is the trough. The wavelength is measured from crest to crest. The wave height is measured from the trailing trough to the peak of the crest. The wave frequency refers to the number of wave crests passing a designated point each second. A wave period is the time it takes for a wave crest to reach the point of the wave crest of the previous wave. The energy in the wave runs into the shallow sea floor. This causes the wave to become steeper and then fall over, or break.

Tides

The gravitational pull of the Sun and Moon causes the oceans to rise and fall each day, creating high and low tides. Most areas have two high tides and two low tides per day. Because the Moon is closer to the Earth than the Sun, its gravitational pull is much greater. The water on the side of the Earth that is closest to the Moon and the water on the opposite side experience high tide. The two low tides occur on the other sides. This changes as the Moon revolves around the Earth. Tidal range is the measurement of the height difference between low and high tide. Tidal range also changes with the location of the Sun and Moon throughout the year, creating spring and neap tides. When all these bodies are aligned, the combined gravitational pull is greater and the tidal range is also greater. This is what creates the spring tide. The neap tide is when the tidal range is at its lowest, which occurs when the Sun and Moon are not at right angles.

Carbon cycle of the ocean

The carbon and nutrient cycles of the ocean are processes that are due in part to the deep currents, mixing, and upwelling that occur in the ocean. Carbon dioxide (CO_2) from the atmosphere is dissolved into the ocean at higher latitudes and distributed to the denser deep water. Where upwelling occurs, CO_2 is brought back to the surface and emitted into the tropical air. Phytoplankton are typically single-celled organisms that are nourished by the Sun. They are photosynthetic autotrophs, meaning they convert water, carbon dioxide, and solar energy into food. They drift with the currents, produce oxygen as a byproduct, and serve as a food source. Zooplankton feed on phytoplankton. Zooplankton are heterotrophic organisms, meaning they do not synthesize their own food. Zooplankton can be single-celled creatures or much larger organisms, such as jellyfish, mollusks, and crustaceans.

Chemical composition of seawater

Salinity is a measure of the amount of dissolved salts in ocean water. It is defined in terms of conductivity. Salinity is influenced by the geologic formations in the area, with igneous formations leading to lower salinity and sedimentary formations leading to higher salinity. Dryer areas with greater rates of evaporation also have higher salt concentrations. Areas where fresh water mixes with ocean water have lower salt concentrations. Hydrogen and oxygen make up about 96.5% of sea water. The major constituents of the dissolved solids of sea water at an atomic level are chlorine (55.3%), sodium (30.8%), magnesium (3.7%), sulfur (2.6%), calcium (1.2%), and potassium (1.1%). The salinity of ocean water is fairly constant, ranging from 34.60 to 34.80 parts per thousand, which is 200 parts per million. Measuring variation on this small of a scale requires instruments that are accurate to about one part per million.

Shoreline and coastal processes

The area where land meets the sea is called the shoreline. This marks the average position of the ocean. Longshore currents create longshore drift or transport (also called beach drift). This is when ocean waves move toward a beach at an angle, which moves water along the coast. Sediment is eroded from some areas and deposited in others. In this way, it is moved along the beach. Rip currents are strong, fast currents that occur when part of longshore current moves away from the beach. Hard, man-made structures built perpendicular to the beach tend to trap sand on the up-current side. Erosion occurs on the down-current side. Features formed by the sediment deposited by waves include spits, bay-mouth bars, tombolos, barrier islands, and buildups. Sand is composed of weather-resistant, granular materials like quartz and orthoclase. In some locations, it is composed of rock and basalt.

<u>Beaches</u>

Weathering erodes the parent material of beaches, rock and soil, into sand, which is typically quartz. Other parts of the soil such as clay and silt are deposited in areas of the continental shelf. The larger sand particles get deposited in the form of a beach. This includes a near shore, which is underwater, a fore shore, the area typically considered the beach, and a back shore. The offshore starts about 5 meters from the shoreline and extends to about 20 meters. The beach also includes wet and dry parts and a fore dune and rear dune. Waves typically move sand from the sea to the beach, and gravity and wave action move it back again. Wind gradually pushes sand particles uphill in a jumping motion called saltation. Sand stays deposited in the form of dunes and the dunes appear as if they roll backward. Storms can both erode a beach and provide additional deposition.

Tilt of the Earth and seasons

The tilt of the Earth on its axis is 23.5°. This tilt causes the seasons and affects the temperature because it affects the amount of Sun the area receives. When the Northern or Southern Hemispheres are tilted toward the Sun, the hemisphere tilted toward the sun experiences summer and the other hemisphere experiences winter. This reverses as the Earth revolves around the Sun. Fall and spring occur between the two extremes. The equator gets the same amount of sunlight every day of the year, about 12 hours, and doesn't experience seasons. Both poles have days during the winter when they are tilted away from the Sun and receive no daylight. The opposite effect occurs during the summer. There are 24 hours of daylight and no night. The summer solstice, the day with the most amount of sunlight, occurs on June 21st in the Northern Hemisphere and on December 21st in the Southern Hemisphere. The winter solstice, the day with the least amount of sunlight, occurs on December 21st in the Northern Hemisphere and on June 21st in the Southern Hemisphere.

Tropospheric circulation

Most weather takes place in the troposphere. Air circulates in the atmosphere by convection and in various types of "cells." Air near the equator is warmed by the Sun and rises. Cool air rushes under it, and the higher, warmer air flows toward Earth's poles. At the poles, it cools and descends to the surface. It is now under the hot air, and flows back to the equator. Air currents coupled with ocean currents move heat around the planet, creating winds, weather, and climate. Winds can change direction with the seasons. For example, in Southeast Asia and India, summer monsoons are caused by air being heated by the Sun. This air rises, draws moisture from the ocean, and causes daily rains. In winter, the air cools, sinks, pushes the moist air away, and creates dry weather.

Weather, climate, and meteorology

Meteorology is the study of the atmosphere, particularly as it pertains to forecasting the weather and understanding its processes. Weather is the condition of the atmosphere at any given moment. Most weather occurs in the troposphere. Weather includes changing events such as clouds, storms, and temperature, as well as more extreme events such as tornadoes, hurricanes, and blizzards.

Climate refers to the average weather for a particular area over time, typically at least 30 years. Latitude is an indicator of climate. Changes in climate occur over long time periods.

Common weather phenomena and meteorological measuring equipment

Common atmospheric conditions that are frequently measured are temperature, precipitation, wind, and humidity. These weather conditions are often measured at permanently fixed weather stations so weather data can be collected and compared over time and by region. Measurements may also be taken by ships, buoys, and underwater instruments. Measurements may also be taken under special circumstances. The measurements taken include temperature, barometric pressure, humidity, wind speed, wind direction, and precipitation. Usually, the following instruments are used: A thermometer is used for measuring temperature; a barometer is used for measuring barometric/air pressure; a hygrometer is used for measuring humidity; an anemometer is used for measuring wind speed; a weather vane is used for measuring wind direction; and a rain gauge is used for measuring precipitation.

Clouds

Clouds form when air cools and warm air is forced to give up some of its water vapor because it can no longer hold it. This vapor condenses and forms tiny droplets of water or ice crystals called clouds. Particles, or aerosols, are needed for water vapor to form water droplets. These are called condensation nuclei. Clouds are created by surface heating, mountains and terrain, rising air masses, and weather fronts. Clouds precipitate, returning the water they contain to Earth. Clouds can also create atmospheric optics. They can scatter light, creating colorful phenomena such as rainbows, colorful sunsets, and the green flash phenomenon.

<u>High, middle, and low cloud types</u>

Most clouds can be classified according to the altitude of their base above Earth's surface. High clouds occur at altitudes between 5,000 and 13,000 meters. Middle clouds occur at altitudes between 2,000 and 7,000 meters. Low clouds occur from the Earth's surface to altitudes of 2,000 meters. Types of high clouds include cirrus (Ci), thin wispy mare's tails that consist of ice; cirrocumulus (Cc), small, pillow-like puffs that often appear in rows; and cirrostratus (Cs), thin, sheetlike clouds that often cover the entire sky. Types of middle clouds include altocumulus (Ac), gray-white clouds that consist of liquid water; and altostratus (As), grayish or blue-gray clouds that span the sky. Types of low clouds include stratus (St), gray and fog-like clouds consisting of water droplets that take up the whole sky; stratocumulus (Sc), low-lying, lumpy gray clouds; and nimbostratus (Ns), dark gray clouds with uneven bases that indicate rain or snow. Two types of clouds, cumulus (Cu) and cumulonimbus (Cb), are capable of great vertical growth. They can start at a wide range of altitudes, from the Earth's surface to altitudes of 13,000 meters.

Latitude, longitude, and equator

For the purposes of tracking time and location, the Earth is divided into sections with imaginary lines. Lines that run vertically around the globe through the poles are lines of longitude, sometimes called meridians. The Prime Meridian is the longitudinal reference point of 0. Longitude is measured in 15-degree increments toward the east or west. Degrees are further divided into 60 minutes, and each minute is divided into 60 seconds. Lines of latitude run horizontally around the Earth parallel to the equator, which is the 0 reference point and the widest point of the Earth. Latitude is the distance north or south from the equator, and is also measured in degrees, minutes, and seconds.

Latitudinal variation and corresponding ecosystems

Latitude is a measurement of the distance from the equator. The distance from the equator indicates how much solar radiation a particular area receives. The equator receives more sunlight, while polar areas receive less. The Earth tilts slightly on its rotational axis. This tilt determines the seasons and affects weather. There are eight biomes or ecosystems with particular climates that are associated with latitude. Those in the high latitudes, which get the least sunlight, are tundra and taiga. Those in the mid latitudes are grassland, temperate forest, and chaparral. Those in latitudes closest to the equator are the warmest. The biomes are desert and tropical rain forest. The eighth biome is the ocean, which is unique because it consists of water and spans the entire globe. Insolation refers to incoming solar radiation. Diurnal variations refer to the daily changes in insolation. The greatest insolation occurs at noon.

Tropic of Cancer, Tropic of Capricorn, and Antarctic and Arctic Circles

The Tropic of Cancer is located at 23.5 degrees north. The Sun is directly overhead at noon on June 21st in the Tropic of Cancer, which marks the beginning of summer in the Northern Hemisphere. The Tropic of Capricorn is located at 23.5 degrees south. The Sun is directly overhead at noon on December 21st in the Tropic of Capricorn, which marks the beginning of winter in the Northern Hemisphere. The Arctic Circle is located at 66.5 degrees north, and marks the start of when the Sun is not visible above the horizon. This occurs on December 21st, the same day the Sun is directly over the Tropic of Capricorn. The Antarctic Circle is located at 66.5 degrees south, and marks the start of when the Sun is not visible above the horizon. This occurs on June 21st, which marks the beginning of winter in the Southern Hemisphere and is when the Sun is directly over the Tropic of Cancer.

Winds and global wind belts

Winds are the result of air moving by convection. Masses of warm air rise, and cold air sweeps into their place. The warm air also moves, cools, and sinks. The term "prevailing wind" refers to the wind that usually blows in an area in a single direction. Dominant winds are the winds with the highest speeds. Belts or bands that run latitudinally and blow in a specific direction are associated with convection cells. Hadley cells are formed directly north and south of the equator. The Farrell cells occur at about 30° to 60°. The jet stream runs between the Farrell cells and the polar cells. At the higher and lower latitudes, the direction is easterly. At mid latitudes, the direction is westerly. From the North Pole to the south, the surface winds are Polar High Easterlies, Subpolar Low Westerlies, Subtropical High or Horse Latitudes, North-East Trade winds, Equatorial Low or Doldrums, South-East Trades, Subtropical High or Horse Latitudes, Subpolar Low Easterlies, and Polar High.

Local atmospheric variations

Terrain affects several local atmospheric conditions, including temperature, wind speed, and wind direction. When there are land forms, heating of the ground can be greater than the heating of the surrounding air than it would be at the same altitude above sea level. This creates a thermal low in the region and amplifies any existing thermal lows. It also changes the wind circulation. Terrain such as hills and valleys increase friction between the air and the land, which disturbs the air flow. This physical block deflects the wind, and the resulting air flow is called a barrier jet. Just as the heating of the land and air affect sea and land breezes along the coast, rugged terrain affects the wind circulation between mountains and valleys.

Relative humidity, absolute humidity, and dew point temperature

Humidity refers to water vapor contained in the air. The amount of moisture contained in air depends upon its temperature. The higher the air temperature, the more moisture it can hold. These higher levels of moisture are associated with higher humidity. Absolute humidity refers to the total amount of moisture air is capable of holding at a certain temperature. Relative humidity is the ratio of water vapor in the air compared to the amount the air is capable of holding at its current temperature. As temperature decreases, absolute humidity stays the same and relative humidity increases. A hygrometer is a device used to measure humidity. The dew point is the temperature at which water vapor condenses into water at a particular humidity.

Precipitation

After clouds reach the dew point, precipitation occurs. Precipitation can take the form of a liquid or a solid. It is known by many names, including rain, snow, ice, dew, and frost. Liquid forms of precipitation include rain and drizzle. Rain or drizzle that freezes on contact is known as freezing rain or freezing drizzle. Solid or frozen forms of precipitation include snow, ice needles or diamond dust, sleet or ice pellets, hail, and graupel or snow pellets. Virga is a form of precipitation that evaporates before reaching the ground. It usually looks like sheets or shafts falling from a cloud. The amount of rainfall is measured with a rain gauge. Intensity can be measured according to how fast precipitation is falling or by how severely it limits visibility. Precipitation plays a major role in the water cycle since it is responsible for depositing much of the Earth's fresh water.

Air masses

Air masses are large volumes of air in the troposphere of the Earth. They are categorized by their temperature and by the amount of water vapor they contain. Arctic and Antarctic air masses are cold, polar air masses are cool, and tropical and equatorial air masses are hot. Other types of air masses include maritime and monsoon, both of which are moist and unstable. There are also continental and superior air masses, which are dry. A weather front separates two masses of air of different densities. It is the principal cause of meteorological phenomena. Air masses are quickly and easily affected by the land they are above. They can have certain characteristics, and then develop new ones when they get blown over a different area.

Bergeron classification system

The Bergeron classification system uses three sets of letters to identify the following characteristics of air masses: moisture content, thermal characteristics from where they originated, and the stability of the atmosphere. The first, moisture content, uses the following letters: "c" represents the dry continental air masses and "m" stands for the moist maritime air masses. The second set of abbreviations are as follows: "T" indicates the air mass is tropical in origin; "P" indicates the air mass is polar in origin; "A" indicates the air mass is Antarctic in origin; "M" stands for monsoon; "E" indicates the air mass is equatorial in origin; and "S" is used to represent superior air, which is dry air formed by a downward motion. The last set of symbols provides an indicator of the stability of the mass. "K" indicates the mass is colder than the ground below it, while "w" indicates the mass is warmer than the ground. For example, cP is a continental polar air mass, while cPk is a polar air mass blowing over the Gulf Stream, which is warmer than the mass.

High and low-pressure systems

The concept of atmospheric pressure involves the idea that air exerts a force. An imaginary column of air 1 square inch in size rising through the atmosphere would exert a force of 14.7 pounds per square inch (psi). Both temperature and altitude affect atmospheric pressure. Low and high pressure systems tend to want to equalize. Air tends to move from areas of high pressure to areas of low pressure. When air moves into a low pressure system, the air that was there gets pushed up, creating lower temperatures and pressures. Water vapor condenses and forms clouds and possibly rain and snow. A barometer is used to measure air pressure.

Weather fronts and weather maps

A weather front is the area between two differing masses of air that affects weather. Frontal movements are influenced by the jet stream and other high winds. Movements are determined by the type of front. Cold fronts move up to twice as fast as warm ones. It is in the turbulent frontal area that commonplace and dramatic weather events take place. This area also creates temperature changes. Weather phenomena include rain, thunderstorms, high winds, tornadoes, cloudiness, clear skies, and hurricanes. Different fronts can be plotted on weather maps using a set of designated symbols. Surface weather maps can also include symbols representing clouds, rain, temperature, air pressure, and fair weather.

Cold, warm, stationary, and occluded fronts

A cold front is a mass of cold air, usually fast moving and dense, that moves into a warm air front, producing clouds. This often produces a temperature drop and rain, hail (frozen rain), thunder, and lightning. A warm front is pushed up by a fast moving cold front. It is often associated with high wispy clouds, such as cirrus and cirrostratus clouds. A stationary front forms when a warm and cold front meet, but neither is strong enough to move the other. Winds blowing parallel to the fronts keep the front stationary. The front may remain in the same place for days until the wind direction changes and both fronts become a single warm or cold front. In other cases, the entire front dissipates. An occluded front is when a cold front pushes into a warm front. The warm air rises and the two masses of cool air join. These types of fronts often occur in areas of low atmospheric pressure.

Front-related weather phenomena

The following are front-related weather phenomena:

- Shearline: This evolves from a stationary front that has gotten smaller. Wind direction shifts over a short distance.
- Dry line or dew point line: This separates two warm air masses of differing moisture content. At lower altitudes, the moist air mass wedges under the drier air. At higher altitudes, the dry air wedges under the moist air. This is a frequent occurrence in the Midwest and Canada, where the dry air of the Southwest and the moister air of the Gulf of Mexico meet. This can lead to extreme weather events, including tornadoes and thunderstorms.
- Squall line: Severe thunderstorms can form at the front of or ahead of a cold front. In some cases, severe thunderstorms can also outrun cold fronts. A squall line can produce extreme weather in the form of heavy rain, hail, lightning, strong winds, tornadoes, and waterspouts.
- Tropical waves or easterly waves: These are atmospheric troughs or areas of low air pressure that travel westward in the tropics, causing clouds and thunderstorms.

Frontal systems on weather maps

Cold fronts are represented on weather maps as a blue line. Solid blue triangles are used to indicate the direction of movement. Warm fronts are represented with a red line. Solid red semi-circles are used to indicate the direction of the front. The cold and warm front symbols are merged and alternated to point in opposite directions to indicate a stationary front. An occluded front is represented by a purple line with alternating solid purple triangles and semi-circles. A surface trough is represented by an orange dashed line. A squall or shear line is represented by a red line. Two dots and a dash are alternated to form the line. A dry line is represented by an orange line with semi-circles in outline form. A tropical wave is represented by a straight orange line. An "L" is used to indicate an area of low atmospheric pressure and an "H" is used to indicate an area of high atmospheric pressure.

Short and long-term weather forecasting

Short and long-term weather forecasting is important because the day-to-day weather greatly affects humans and human activity. Severe weather and natural events can cause devastating harm to humans, property, and sources of livelihood, such as crops. The persistence method of forecasting can be used to create both short and long-term forecasts in areas that change very little or change slowly. It assumes that the weather tomorrow will be similar to the weather today. Barometric pressure is measured because a change in air pressure can indicate the arrival of a cold front that could lead to precipitation. Long-term forecasts based on climate data are useful to help people prepare for seasonal changes and severe events such as hurricanes.

Hydrologic cycle

The hydrologic, or water, cycle refers to water movement on, above, and in the Earth. Water can be in any one of its three states during different phases of the cycle. The three states of water are liquid water, frozen ice, and water vapor. Processes involved in the hydrologic cycle include precipitation, canopy interception, snow melt, runoff, infiltration, subsurface flow, evaporation, sublimation, advection, condensation, and transpiration. Precipitation occurs when condensed water vapor falls to Earth. Examples include rain, fog drip, and various forms of snow, hail, and sleet. Canopy interception occurs when precipitation lands on plant foliage instead of falling to the ground and evaporating. Snowmelt is runoff produced by melting snow. Infiltration occurs when water flows from the surface into the ground. Subsurface flow refers to water that flows underground. Evaporation occurs when water in a liquid state changes to a gas. Sublimation occurs when water in a solid state (such as snow or ice) changes to water vapor without going through a liquid phase. Advection is the movement of water through the atmosphere. Condensation occurs when water vapor changes to liquid water. Transpiration occurs when water vapor is released from plants into the air.

Earth's atmosphere

The atmosphere consists of 78% nitrogen, 21% oxygen, and 1% argon. It also includes traces of water vapor, carbon dioxide and other gases, dust particles, and chemicals from Earth. The atmosphere becomes thinner the farther it is from the Earth's surface. It becomes difficult to breathe at about 3 km above sea level. The atmosphere gradually fades into space. Earth's atmosphere has five main layers. From lowest to highest, these are the troposphere, the stratosphere, the mesosphere, the thermosphere, and the exosphere. Between each pair of layers is a transition layer called a pause.

The lowest layer of the atmosphere is called the troposphere. Its thickness varies at the poles and the equator, varying from about 7 to 17 km. This is where most weather occurs. The troposphere includes the tropopause, which is the transitional layer of the stratosphere. Energy from Earth's surface is transferred to the troposphere. Temperature decreases with altitude in this layer. The stratosphere is next, and continues to an elevation of about 51 km. In the stratosphere, the temperature is inverted, meaning that it increases with altitude. The stratosphere includes the ozone layer, which helps block ultraviolet light from the Sun. The stratopause is the transitional layer to the mesosphere. The mesosphere extends from the stratosphere to an elevation of about 81 km. It is the coldest layer and is where meteors tend to ablate. The temperature of the mesosphere decreases with height. It is considered the coldest place on Earth, and has an average temperature of -85 degrees Celsius. The next layer is the thermosphere. It is where the International Space Station orbits. Temperature increases with altitude in the thermosphere, which includes the thermopause. Just past the thermosphere is the exobase, the base layer of the exosphere. The exosphere is the outermost layer, extends to 10,000 km, and mainly consists of hydrogen and helium. Beyond the five main layers are the ionosphere, homosphere, heterosphere, and magnetosphere.

Other layers above the surface of the Earth

The ozone layer, although contained within the stratosphere, is determined by ozone (O_3) concentrations. It absorbs the majority of ultraviolet light from the Sun. The ionosphere is part of both the exosphere and the thermosphere. It is characterized by the fact that it is a plasma, a partially ionized gas in which free electrons and positive ions are attracted to each other, but are too energetic to remain fixed as a molecule. It starts at about 50 km above Earth's surface and goes to 1,000 km. It affects radio wave transmission and auroras. The ionosphere pushes against the inner edge of the Earth's magnetosphere, which is the highly magnetized, non-spherical region around the Earth. The homosphere encompasses the troposphere, stratosphere, and mesosphere. Gases in the homosphere are considered well mixed. In the heterosphere, the distance that particles can move without colliding is large. As a result, gases are stratified according to their molecular weights. Heavier gases such as oxygen and nitrogen occur near the bottom of the heterosphere, while hydrogen, the lightest element, is found at the top.

Practice Test

Practice Questions

1. Which of the following statements correctly describes a similarity or difference between rocks and minerals?

a. Minerals may contain traces of organic compounds, while rocks do not.
b. Rocks are classified by their formation and the minerals they contain, while minerals are classified by their chemical composition and physical properties.
c. Both rocks and minerals can be polymorphs.
d. Both rocks and minerals may contain mineraloids.

2. Which of the following is the best description of mineraloids?

a. Mineraloids are organic compounds found in rocks.
b. Mineraloids are inorganic solids containing two or more minerals with different crystalline structures.
c. Mineraloids are inorganic solids containing one or more minerals with the same crystalline structure.
d. Mineraloids are minerals that lack a crystalline structure.

3. All of the following are branches of petrology EXCEPT:

a. Metamorphic petrology.
b. Igneous petrology.
c. Mineralogical petrology.
d. Sedimentary petrology.

4. Which of the following is NOT one of the five major physical properties of minerals?

a. Chemical composition
b. Hardness
c. Luster
d. Streak

5. Which of these minerals would have the lowest score on the Mohs scale?

a. Gypsum
b. Fluorite
c. Talc
d. Diamond

6. A mineral's true color is observed by:

a. Conducting a streak test on white paper.
b. Conducting a streak test on unglazed porcelain tile.
c. Inspecting the mineral's outer surface.
d. Shining a light on the mineral to inspect its luster.

7. Galena, pyrite, and magnetite are examples of minerals with which of the following types of luster?

a. Pearly
b. Greasy
c. Adamantine
d. Metallic

8. According to the Dana classification system, gold, silver, and copper belong to which class?

a. Organic
b. Elemental
c. Oxide
d. Sulfide

9. According to the Dana classification system, minerals that contain the anion SO_4^{2-} are part of which chemical class?

a. Sulfate
b. Sulfite
c. Halide
d. Phosphate

10. Minerals that form on the sea floor from discarded shells are most likely part of which chemical class?

a. Sulfate
b. Organic
c. Carbonate
d. Silicate

11. The lithification process results in the formation of which of the following types of rocks?

a. Sedimentary
b. Intrusive igneous
c. Extrusive igneous
d. Metamorphic

12. Which of the following types of igneous rock solidifies deepest beneath the Earth's surface?

a. Hypabyssal
b. Plutonic
c. Volcanic
d. Detrital

13. Which of the following factors directly contributes to soil erosion?

a. Air pollution from cars and factories
b. Use of pesticides
c. Deforestation and overgrazing
d. Water pollution caused by excess sedimentation

14. Physical weathering of rocks can be caused by all of the following EXCEPT:

a. The freezing and thawing of water on the surface of rocks.
b. Changes in temperature.
c. Oxidation.
d. Changes in pressure due to the removal of overlying rocks.

15. Which of the following is NOT an example of chemical weathering of rocks?

a. Highly acidic rainwater causes dissolution of rocks.
b. Minerals that comprise rocks take on water, causing them to enlarge and creating fractures within the rocks.
c. Salt water penetrates fractures in rocks and leaves behind salt crystals that cause fractures.
d. Iron molecules in rocks react with atmospheric oxygen, which causes oxidation.

16. Which of the following lists places several phases of the sedimentary cycle in the correct order?

a. Erosion, weathering, transportation, deposition
b. Weathering, erosion, deposition, transportation
c. Weathering, deposition, erosion, transportation
d. Weathering, erosion, transportation, deposition

17. Which of the following is required for the process of diagenesis (also called lithification)?

a. Magma
b. Water
c. Wind
d. Sulfur

18. Nondetrital sedimentary rock is produced by:

a. Chemical precipitation.
b. Cooling of magma just below the Earth's surface.
c. Physical weathering processes.
d. Weathering of igneous rock.

19. Leaching in the "A" soil horizon results from:

a. The accumulation of cations in the "B" horizon.
b. The accumulation of cations in the "O" horizon.
c. Contact with acid solutions generated in the "O" horizon.
d. Contact with acid solutions generated in the "B" horizon.

20. Which of the following statements is true of rocks such as olivine that are found at the top of Bowen's reaction series?

a. They are classified as metamorphic.
b. They weather more quickly than rocks found lower in the series.
c. They crystallize at lower temperatures than rocks found at the bottom of the series.
d. None of the above

21. Metamorphic rock is produced when which of the following undergoes profound changes as a result of exposure to intense pressure and heat?

a. A batholith
b. A protolith
c. A subduction zone
d. A volcano

22. All of the following are examples of metamorphic rocks EXCEPT:

a. Granite.
b. Quartzite.
c. Slate.
d. Marble.

23. When metamorphic rock is stressed unevenly during recrystallization, it can result in:

a. Foliation.
b. Contact metamorphism.
c. Regional metamorphism.
d. Extrusion.

24. Which of the following statements correctly describes a distinction between regional and contact metamorphism?

a. Regional metamorphism results from intense heat, while contact metamorphism is caused by extreme pressure.
b. Regional metamorphism results from extreme pressure, while contact metamorphism is caused by intense heat.
c. Regional metamorphism occurs when magma is injected into surrounding rock, while contact metamorphism occurs when a large area of rock is subjected to intense heat and pressure.
d. Regional metamorphism occurs when a large area of rock is subjected to intense heat and pressure, while contact metamorphism occurs when magma is injected into surrounding rock.

25. When two tectonic plates are moving laterally in opposing directions, this is called a:

a. Transformational boundary.
b. Compressional boundary.
c. Oppositional boundary.
d. Lateral boundary.

26. Which of the following statements correctly describes a difference between the lithosphere and the asthenosphere?

a. The asthenosphere is comprised of atmospheric gas, while the lithosphere is composed of liquids and solids.
b. The asthenosphere is hotter and more fluid than the lithosphere.
c. The lithosphere is hotter and has a different chemical composition than the asthenosphere.
d. Heat is transferred through conduction in the asthenosphere, while it is transferred through convection in the lithosphere.

27. The most recently formed parts of the Earth's crust can be found at:

a. Subduction zones.
b. Compressional boundaries.
c. Extensional boundaries.
d. Mid-ocean ridges.

28. When an earthquake occurs, the "shaking" that is observed results directly from:

a. Static deformation.
b. Seismic waves.
c. Compression waves.
d. Continental drift.

29. Which of the following events immediately precedes a volcanic eruption?

a. A batholith forms beneath the Earth's surface.
b. Magma fills vertical and horizontal fractures in the Earth's crust, creating sills and dykes.
c. An oceanic plate is subducted by a continental plate.
d. A dyke reaches the Earth's surface and a plume passes through it.

30. Cinder cone volcanoes are created by:

a. A series of explosive eruptions.
b. Gradual eruptions over time.
c. A combination of both explosive and gradual eruptions over time.
d. None of the above

31. Island chains like the Hawaiian or Midway Islands are created when:

a. Tectonic plates move apart and magma rises to the surface.
b. The subduction process creates magma, which rises above the ocean's surface to form islands.
c. Underwater earthquakes produce mountains that protrude above the water's surface.
d. A tectonic plate gradually moves over a fixed plume of magma that rises from the mantle.

32. Which of the following is true of a volcano that is thought to be dormant?

a. It will probably never erupt again, and it is quite safe for people to live near its base.
b. It is expected to erupt some time again in the future, but danger is not imminent.
c. It is expected to erupt soon, and evacuation should be commenced.
d. It is a shield volcano that is erupting, but people living near the volcano should not expect their lives to be significantly disrupted.

33. The mountain in Figure 1 has the oldest rock in its core and the youngest rock in its outer layers. Which of the following terms best describes the mountain?

a. Syncline
b. Anticline
c. Fault-block
d. Graben

Figure 1.

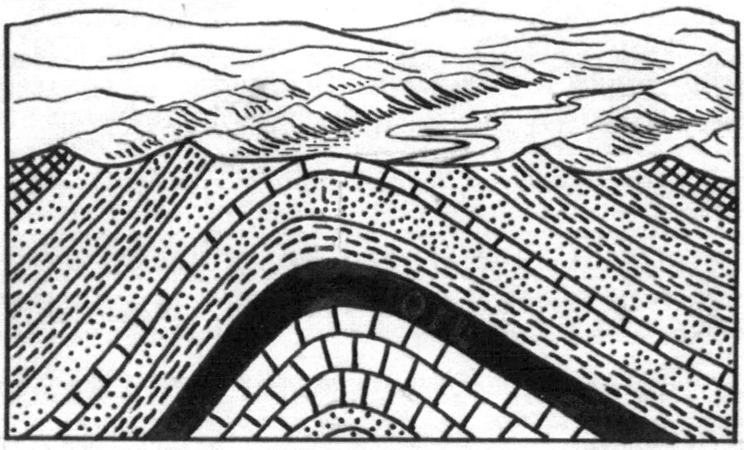

34. When fault-block mountains like those in the Western United States are formed, sections that are lifted by tensional forces are called:

a. Antiforms.
b. Faces.
c. Horsts.
d. Rifts.

35. Which of the following is thought to be a direct result of the Dynamo Effect?

a. The motion of tectonic plates over the mantle
b. The heating of the Earth's atmosphere
c. The production of the Earth's magnetic field
d. None of the above

36. The Earth's magnetic field protects it from:

a. Excess heat from the Sun.
b. Radio waves from black holes.
c. Solar wind.
d. Impacts from space debris.

37. In 1912, Alfred Wegener proposed that:

a. The Earth's magnetic poles have reversed several times throughout history.
b. Tectonic plates move because of convection currents in the mantle.
c. Mountains are formed by tectonic plates pushing against one another.
d. The continents once formed a single land mass, but have since drifted apart.

38. The Richter scale determines the magnitude of an earthquake by:

a. Comparing its destructiveness to that of other earthquakes.
b. Measuring the amount of seismic energy it releases.
c. Ascertaining the farthest distance from the epicenter at which the earthquake can be felt.
d. Measuring the depth of the earthquake.

39. An earthquake with a Richter magnitude of 1.5 can be expected to have which of the following effects on an urban area with high standards for building construction?

a. The earthquake will probably not be felt, and will not cause damage.
b. There may be slight damage to well-constructed buildings over a small area.
c. There will be serious damage to well-constructed buildings over a large area.
d. There will be catastrophic damage and many people will be injured.

40. The process that causes lithospheric plates to move over the surface of the mantle is called:

a. Conduction.
b. Convection.
c. Tension.
d. Subduction.

41. Which of the following statements correctly describes the relationship between temperature and density in water?

a. As the temperature of liquid water decreases, density decreases monotonically.
b. As the temperature of frozen water (ice) increases, density decreases monotonically.
c. Water in the solid state generally has a higher density than water in the liquid state.
d. Water in the liquid state generally has a higher density than water in the solid state.

42. Water's specific heat capacity is second only to that of ammonia. This means that:

a. Water vaporizes at a higher temperature than ammonia.
b. It takes more energy to increase the temperature of ammonia than it does to increase the temperature of water.
c. Water is always denser than ammonia.
d. Water is only denser than ammonia at higher temperatures.

43. Water that evaporates from oceans can precipitate over land due to the process of:

a. Transpiration.
b. Advection.
c. Sublimation.
d. Interception.

44. Water is likely to have the shortest residence time in which of the following types of reservoirs?

a. A glacier
b. A lake
c. A river
d. The atmosphere

45. When water changes directly from a solid to a gas, skipping the liquid state, this is called:

a. Evapotranspiration.
b. Condensation.
c. Sublimation.
d. Runoff.

46. The main manmade cause of "dead zones" in portions of oceans and lakes that normally host abundant aquatic life is:

a. Evaporation.
b. Invasive species.
c. Use of chemical fertilizers.
d. Global warming.

47. The majority of the solar energy that reaches Earth is absorbed by:

a. Glaciers.
b. Landmasses.
c. Oceans.
d. The Earth's atmosphere.

48. The majority of weather phenomena occur in which part of the Earth's atmosphere?

a. Troposphere
b. Stratosphere
c. Hydrosphere
d. Ionosphere

49. According to the Köppen Climate Classification System, regions with continental climates are most commonly found:

a. In the interior regions of large landmasses.
b. Near the equator.
c. Near the Earth's poles.
d. In places with high temperatures year-round.

50. Tropical climate zones are characterized by:

a. Extreme temperature variations between night and day.
b. Extreme temperature variations between seasons.
c. Frequent rainfall.
d. All of the above

51. Which of the following is a true statement about the Earth's oceans?

a. Oceans comprise about 50 percent of the Earth's surface.
b. The deepest point in the ocean is about 6,000 meters below sea level.
c. The ocean is divided geographically into four areas: the Atlantic, Pacific, Mediterranean, and Indian.
d. The ocean's salinity is usually between 34 and 35 parts per thousand, or 200 parts per million.

52. A guyot is defined as:

a. Any undersea mountain more than 1,000 meters high.
b. A seamount with a flattened top.
c. An undersea mountain chain.
d. A trough in the ocean floor.

53. Approximately 96.5 percent of seawater is comprised of:

a. Hydrogen and sodium.
b. Hydrogen and oxygen.
c. Oxygen and sodium.
d. Chlorine and sodium.

54. Which of the following statements correctly describes a difference between surface and subsurface ocean currents?

a. Subsurface currents are caused only by temperature variations, while surface currents are caused by changes in air pressure.
b. Subsurface currents are caused by temperature and density variations, while surface currents are caused by changes in air pressure.
c. Subsurface currents are caused by temperature and density variations, while surface currents are caused by wind.
d. Surface currents are caused by changes in air temperature, while subsurface currents are caused by changes in water temperature.

55. The Coriolis effect in the Earth's oceans is caused by:

a. The Earth's rotation.
b. The Earth's magnetic field.
c. Variations in the density of seawater.
d. The Gulf Stream.

56. Which of the following statements correctly describes an effect of the Gulf Stream?

a. It increases humidity along North America's west coast.
b. It makes the climate of South America colder.
c. It makes the climate of Northern Europe warmer.
d. It makes the climate of the Caribbean milder and less humid.

57. Thermohaline circulation is caused by:

a. Temperature differences between seawater only.
b. Salinity differences between seawater only.
c. Variations in seawater density caused by both temperature and salinity differences.
d. None of the above

58. When cold, nutrient-rich water is allowed to rise to the surface because winds parallel to a landmass's coast blow the surface water towards the open sea, this is called:

a. Ekman transport.
b. The Coriolis effect.
c. Upwelling.
d. Downwelling.

59. The frequency of ocean waves is measured by:

a. The distance between a wave's crest and trough.
b. The distance between the crests of two subsequent waves.
c. The time between two subsequent wave crests.
d. The number of wave crests that pass a given point each second.

60. When the accumulation of snow and ice exceeds ablation, which of the following occurs as a direct result?

a. An iceberg breaks free from a glacier.
b. A glacier gradually forms.
c. A glacier slowly erodes.
d. A lake forms within a glacier.

61. The Cretaceous-Tertiary Event, during which non-avian dinosaurs became extinct, occurred approximately how long ago?

a. 10,000 years ago
b. 15.5 million years ago
c. 38 million years ago
d. 65.5 million years ago

62. Which of the following techniques is NOT a radiometric dating process?

a. Potassium-argon dating
b. Stratigraphic dating
c. Uranium-lead dating
d. Chlorine-36 dating

63. In the field of geology, the term "uniformitarianism" refers to the belief that:

a. Catastrophic events like mass extinctions are the main forces that have shaped the Earth.
b. The Earth's crust has not undergone any dramatic changes since its formation.
c. The natural forces that shape the Earth have remained relatively constant over geologic time.
d. The Earth's stratigraphy is more or less uniform at any given geographic location.

64. In the field of stratigraphy, the relative ages of rocks may be determined by examining which of the following types of evidence?

a. The dates the rocks were formed and the ages of fossils deposited within the rocks
b. Evidence of changes in detrital remanent magnetism when the rock was deposited
c. The vertical layering pattern of the rock
d. All of the above

65. Which of the following is an example of an absolute age?

a. A fossil is 37 million years old.
b. A rock is less than 100,000 years old.
c. An organic artifact is between 5,000 and 10,000 years old.
d. All of the above

66. In geochronology, which of the following is the longest time period?

a. An epoch
b. An era
c. An eon
d. An age

67. Which of the following correctly lists the periods that comprise the Mesozoic era, from earliest to most recent?

a. Jurassic, Triassic, Cretaceous
b. Permian, Triassic, Jurassic
c. Triassic, Jurassic, Cretaceous
d. Triassic, Jurassic, Permian

68. In his work, *The Origin of Life*, Alexander Oparin argued that:

a. Life arose spontaneously from other decaying organic matter.
b. Life originated in deep-sea vents.
c. Life arose on Earth through a "primordial soup" that is no longer possible because of atmospheric oxygen.
d. Life emerged as part of an autocatalytic network.

69. According to current theories, the Earth was formed approximately how long ago?

a. 50 million years ago
b. 1.25 billion years ago
c. 4.5 billion years ago
d. 15 billion years ago

70. The most severe mass extinction event in Earth's history was the:

a. Cretaceous-Tertiary Event.
b. Permian-Triassic Event.
c. Ordovician-Silurian Event.
d. Late Devonian Event.

71. Which of the following life forms appeared first on Earth?

a. Eukaryotes
b. Arthropods
c. Prokaryotes
d. Amphibians

72. The Cambrian Explosion is best described as:

a. A great migration of flora and fauna between North and South America that vastly increased biodiversity on both continents.
b. The emergence of multicellular life about one billion years ago.
c. The increase in the pace of evolution ushered in by the emergence of sexual reproduction about 1.2 billion years ago.
d. The dramatic increase in biodiversity that began about 530 million years ago and resulted in the emergence of complex animals over a period of millions of years.

73. Which of the following is considered observational evidence in support of the Big Bang Theory?

a. Expansion in the redshifts of galaxies
b. Measurements of cosmic microwave background radiation
c. Measurements of the distribution of quasars and galaxies
d. All of the above

74. The Cosmological Principle is best described as:

a. An assumption that cannot be tested empirically because it has no observable implications.
b. A scientific hypothesis that has been repeatedly validated in empirical tests.
c. A working assumption that has testable structural consequences.
d. A law of physics that defies empirical testing.

75. Redshift is observed when:

a. A light-emitting object moves away from an observer.
b. A star begins to decrease the amount of light it emits.
c. A light-emitting object moves toward an observer.
d. A magnetic field bends observed light.

76. Which of the following statements best describes the physical structure of the universe?

a. Galaxies are the largest structures in the universe, and they are distributed evenly throughout space.
b. Superclusters are the largest structures in the universe, and they are distributed evenly throughout space.
c. Superclusters are the largest structures in the universe, and they are unevenly distributed so that large voids exist in space.
d. Filaments are the largest structures in the universe, and they surround large, bubble-like voids.

77. Which of the following statements about galaxies is true?

a. Galaxies are the only structures in the universe that do not contain dark matter.
b. Galaxies are gravitationally bound, meaning structures within the galaxy orbit around its center.
c. Galaxies typically contain over one trillion stars.
d. Galaxies are comprised of clusters and superclusters.

78. The structure of the Milky Way galaxy is best described as:

a. Spiral.
b. Starburst.
c. Elliptical.
d. Irregular.

79. The Hertzsprung-Russell (H-R) Diagram is used primarily to:

a. Determine a star's age by comparing its temperature and luminosity.
b. Measure a star's size by estimating its luminosity.
c. Determine a galaxy's luminosity when its size is known.
d. Group galaxies by their morphological types.

80. The distance from the Earth to the Sun is equal to one:

a. Astronomical unit.
b. Light year.
c. Parsec.
d. Arcsecond.

81. The energy radiated by stars is produced by:

a. Neutronicity.
b. Nuclear fusion.
c. Nuclear fission.
d. Gravitational confinement.

82. The stream of charged particles that escape the Sun's gravitational pull is best described by which of the following terms?

a. Solar wind
b. Solar flare
c. Solar radiation
d. Sunspots

83. Which of the following planets in our solar system is NOT a gas giant?

a. Saturn
b. Neptune
c. Venus
d. Jupiter

84. The asteroid belt in our solar system is located between:

a. Earth and Mars.
b. Neptune and Pluto.
c. Uranus and Saturn.
d. Mars and Jupiter.

85. Which of the following is a proposed explanation for the formation of black holes?

a. High-energy collisions
b. Gravitational collapse
c. Accretion of matter
d. A and B

86. A total solar eclipse can be observed only by viewers located:

a. Within the penumbra but outside of the umbra.
b. Within the umbra.
c. Within either the umbra or the penumbra.
d. Outside of the Moon's penumbra.

87. The atomic number of an element is defined by:

a. The total number of protons and electrons it contains.
b. The total number of electrons it contains.
c. The total number of protons it contains.
d. The total number of neutrons it contains.

88. Which of the following statements best describes the main distinction between the isotopes carbon-12 and carbon-13?

a. They have different atomic numbers.
b. They have different mass numbers.
c. They have experienced different degrees of radioactive decay.
d. A and B

89. Which of the following statements is NOT true of electrons?

a. They comprise only a tiny fraction of an atom's mass.
b. They are arranged in levels, and usually occupy the lowest energy level possible.
c. They are negatively charged.
d. They have a substructure that includes a nucleus.

90. Chemical compounds are formed when:

a. Valence electrons from atoms of two different elements are shared or transferred.
b. Valence electrons from multiple atoms of a single element are shared or transferred.
c. The nuclei of two atoms are joined together.
d. The nucleus of an atom is split.

91. The state of matter in which atoms have the strongest bond is:

a. Plasma.
b. Liquid.
c. Solid.
d. Gas.

92. Which of the following statements is true of a closed thermodynamic system?

a. It cannot exchange heat, work, or matter with its surrounding environment.
b. It can exchange heat and work, but not matter, with its surrounding environment.
c. It can exchange heat, but not work or matter, with its surrounding environment.
d. It can exchange matter, but not heat or work, with its surrounding environment.

93. The formula for calculating kinetic energy is:

a. ½ mv2.
b. ½ mv.
c. mgh.
d. mgv.

94. Which law of classical thermodynamics states that energy can neither be created nor destroyed?

a. Zeroth
b. First
c. Second
d. Third

95. James Hutton is best known for:

a. Establishing the first observable evidence for the Big Bang Theory.
b. Suggesting the Third Law of Thermodynamics.
c. Proposing the theory of uniformitarianism.
d. Introducing the Law of Superposition.

96. Which of the following is the correct formula for converting Fahrenheit to Celsius?

a. C = 5/9 (F - 32)
b. C = 9/5 (F - 32)
c. C = 5/9 (F + 32)
d. None of the above

97. A calorimeter is used to measure changes in:

a. Heat.
b. Mass.
c. Weight.
d. Volume.

98. Commercial nuclear reactors generate electricity through the process of:

a. Nuclear fission.
b. Nuclear fusion.
c. Nuclear depletion.
d. Radioactive decay.

99. Which of the following can be inferred based on the results of the regression analysis shown in Figure 2?

a. A change in the independent variable causes a change in the dependent variable.
b. A change in the dependent variable causes a change in the independent variable.
c. There is a weak positive correlation between the two variables.
d. There is a weak negative correlation between the two variables.

Figure 2.

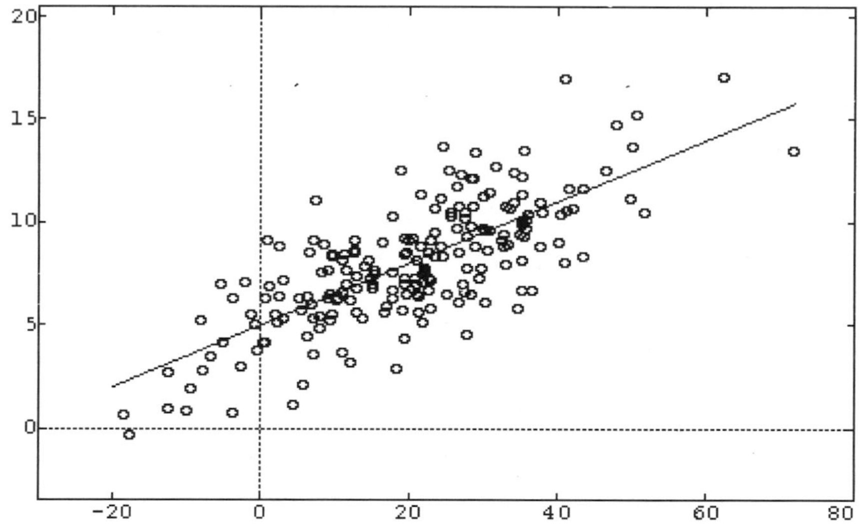

100. Random error could be caused by which of the following problems?

a. Imperfectly calibrated equipment
b. Extraneous disturbances that cannot be controlled
c. Consistent human error in the use of lab equipment
d. Failure to account for a specific variable

Answers and Explanations

1. B: It is true that rocks are classified by their formation and the minerals they contain, while minerals are classified by their chemical composition and physical properties. Answer A is incorrect because rocks may contain traces of organic compounds. Answers C and D are incorrect because only minerals can be polymorphs and only rocks contain mineraloids.

2. D: Mineraloids are best defined as minerals that lack a crystalline structure, and they are typically found in rocks. Inorganic solids containing two or more minerals with different crystalline structures are known as polymorphs.

3. C: Mineralogical petrology is not a branch of petrology. Petrologists study the various categories of rocks, including metamorphic, igneous, and sedimentary. Some petrologists, called experimental petrologists, also study changes in the geochemistry of materials that are exposed to extreme temperatures and pressures. Minerals are studied by mineralogists, not petrologists.

4. A: Chemical composition is not one of the physical properties used to classify minerals. The five major physical properties used to classify minerals are luster, hardness, cleavage, streak, and form. There is a separate classification system based on the chemical composition of minerals.

5. C: On Mohs scale of mineral hardness, talc has the lowest possible score (a one). Diamond is a ten, which is the highest possible score, and gypsum and fluorite have a score of two and four, respectively. Minerals can always scratch minerals that have a Mohs score lower than their own.

6. B: A mineral's true color is observed by conducting a streak test on unglazed porcelain tile. Paper is not appropriate for a streak test because it does not have the correct physical properties. External observation (inspecting the mineral's outer surface) is not sufficient to establish true color since streak tests sometimes reveal a color that is different from the substance's external hue. Finally, the luster test is not used to determine color.

7. D: Galena, pyrite, and magnetite are examples of minerals with a metallic luster. Opal is an example of a mineral with a greasy luster, and diamonds have an adamantine luster. Muscovite and stilbite are examples of minerals with a pearly luster. Other types of luster include dull, silky, waxy, and sub-metallic.

8. B: According to the Dana classification system, gold, silver, and copper belong to the elemental class. Members of the oxide class include chromite and magnetite, and hydrocarbons and acetates are members of the organic class. Sulfide minerals include pyrite and galena.

9. A: According to the Dana system, minerals that contain the anion SO_4^{2-} are part of the sulfate class. Sulfate minerals are typically formed in environments where highly saline water evaporates. Gypsum is an example of a mineral that belongs to the sulfate class.

10. C: Minerals that form on the sea floor from discarded shells are most likely part of the carbonate class. Minerals that form in karst regions and evaporitic settings may also be carbonates. Examples of minerals in the carbonate class include aragonite, dolomite, calcite, and siderite.

11. A: The lithification process results in the formation of sedimentary rocks. During lithification, existing rock is compacted and liquid is squeezed from its pores. Eventually, the rock is cemented together, resulting in sedimentary rock.

12. B: Plutonic, or intrusive, rock forms deep beneath the Earth's surface and cools slowly. Volcanic, or extrusive, rock solidifies at or near the surface. Hypabyssal rock forms below the Earth's surface, but not at a depth as great as plutonic rock. Detrital rock is a type of sedimentary rock.

13. C: Overgrazing and deforestation directly contribute to soil erosion by destroying the natural groundcover that normally prevents soil from being washed and blown away. These activities can ultimately result in desertification, which renders land unsuitable for agriculture.

14. C: Physical weathering of rocks can be caused by changes in temperature and pressure, as well as the freezing and thawing of water on the surfaces of rocks. Oxidation is a chemical process, not a physical one. Therefore, it is considered an example of chemical rather than physical weathering.

15. C: When salt water penetrates fractures in rocks and leaves behind salt crystals that cause the rock to fracture, it is considered physical rather than chemical weathering. Chemical weathering involves changes in the molecules that comprise the rocks, while physical weathering occurs when external factors act on the rock without changing its chemical composition in any way.

16. D: Weathering causes erosion, which often leads to transportation and the deposition of eroded material. After the eroded material is deposited in a new location, lithification proceeds and the sedimentary cycle begins anew.

17. B: Water is a key element in the lithification of sedimentary rock. After it is squeezed from the compressed material, it forms a chemical cement that holds the sedimentary rock in place. This cementation process is followed by recrystallization of the rock when equilibrium is reached.

18. A: Non-detrital sedimentary rock is produced by chemical precipitation. In contrast, detrital sedimentary rocks are comprised of pre-existing rocks, such as quartz, or weathered products of pre-existing rocks, such as clay.

19. C: Leaching in the "A" soil horizon results from contact with acid solutions generated in the "O" horizon, which is the uppermost organic layer of soil. Cations that are leached in the "A" soil horizon accumulate in the "B" soil horizon below.

20. B: Rocks such as olivine that are found at the top of Bowen's reaction series weather more quickly than rocks found lower in the series. This is because rocks high in the series crystallize at higher temperatures than those found lower in the series. This means they are less stable and more susceptible to weathering than rocks that crystallize at lower temperatures, such as quartz.

21. B: Metamorphic rock is produced when a protolith undergoes profound changes after being exposed to extreme heat and pressure. A protolith is any rock that is transformed through this process. The original rock may be sedimentary, igneous, or metamorphic. The extreme heat and pressure that serve as the catalyst for this transformation may be produced by the intrusion of magma or tectonic activity, among other factors.

22. A: Quartzite, marble, and slate are all examples of metamorphic rocks, while granite is one of the most common types of igneous rocks.

23. A: When metamorphic rock is stressed unevenly during recrystallization, it can result in foliation. Foliation is characterized by banded rock, and it occurs when certain types of minerals are reoriented during recrystallization due to uneven shortening or compression of the rock.

24. D: Regional metamorphism occurs when a large area of rock is subjected to intense heat and pressure, while contact metamorphism occurs when magma is injected into surrounding rock, also known as country rock. When contact metamorphism occurs, the rocks closest to the hot magma undergo the greatest changes.

25. A: When two tectonic plates are moving laterally in opposing directions, this is called a transform boundary. When there is friction at transform boundaries and pressure builds up, it can result in shallow earthquakes (usually at a depth of less than 25 meters). California's San Andreas Fault is an example of a transform boundary.

26. B: It is true that the asthenosphere is hotter and more fluid than the lithosphere. The asthenosphere, also called the upper mantle, is the hot, fluid layer of the Earth's mantle upon which the lithosphere, or crust, is situated. Heat is transferred within the asthenosphere through a process called convection, which sometimes causes movement in the tectonic plates that make up the lithosphere.

27. D: The most recently formed parts of the Earth's crust can be found at mid-ocean ridges. New crust forms here when magma erupts from these ridges and pushes pre-existing crust horizontally towards the continental plates. Such ridges include the Mid-Atlantic Ridge and the East Pacific Rise.

28. B: When an earthquake occurs, the "shaking" that is observed is a direct result of seismic waves. Seismic waves are powerful sound waves released when slippage between plates occurs. There are two types of seismic waves: primary, or P-waves, and secondary, or S-waves. P-waves move more quickly than S-waves, and create motion that radiates directly outward from the point of origin. S-waves produce a shearing, or side-to-side, motion.

29. D: A volcano occurs when a dyke (a vertical fracture in the Earth's crust that fills with magma) reaches the Earth's surface and a plume (a spurt of magma) passes through it. Batholiths are large masses of igneous rock that form beneath the Earth's surface, and a sill is a horizontal fracture in the Earth's crust that fills with magma. When an oceanic plate is subducted by a continental plate, it results in the formation of mountain ranges.

30. A: Cinder cone volcanoes are created by a series of explosive eruptions. Gradual eruptions produce shield volcanoes, and composite volcanoes are the result of a combination of gradual and explosive eruptions over time.

31. D: Island chains like the Hawaiian or Midway Islands are created when a tectonic plate gradually moves over a fixed plume of magma that rises from the mantle. When this plume erupts through the Earth's crust, a volcano that rises above the water's surface is formed, which creates an island. The tectonic plate gradually shifts so that the next time the fixed plume erupts, it affects a different point on the plate. This creates another volcanic island near the first one.

32. B: A volcano that is thought to be dormant is expected to erupt some time again in the future, but danger is not imminent. Dormant volcanoes are expected to erupt again in the future because they still show signs of internal volcanic activity. Extinct volcanoes are not expected to erupt again because they show no signs of activity. Active volcanoes are either erupting or about to erupt.

33. B: Since the mountain in Figure 1 has the oldest rock in its core and the youngest rock in its outer layers, it is best described as an anticline. Any mountain that results from a crustal fold and has an upward, convex shape is called an antiform. Mountains in which the rocks are progressively older from the outer layers to the core are anticlines. Synclines have downward, or concave, folds,

and fault-block mountains result when faults in continental crust cause certain sections to lift or tilt. Grabens are a formation associated with fault-block mountains.

34. C: When fault-block mountains such as those in the Western United States are formed, sections that are lifted by tensional forces are called horsts. Blocks that are lowered in elevation are called grabens. The term "rift" refers to the entire area that is affected by the separation of a continental plate.

35. C: The Earth's magnetic field is thought to be produced by the Dynamo Effect. According to this theory, the Earth's rotation combined with the convection of metals within the Earth's core produce electric currents. When these currents flow through an existing magnetic field in the core, this produces a secondary magnetic field which reinforces the primary field and creates a self-sustaining dynamo.

36. C: The Earth's magnetic field protects it from solar wind. Solar wind is a stream of highly-charged radioactive particles that emanate from the Sun, and these particles are deflected by the magnetic field. The magnetic field is shaped like a bowl that covers the side of the Earth facing the Sun. It deflects most solar particles, but some are trapped in the Van Allen belt. Particularly strong bursts of solar wind allow particles to pass through this belt into the Earth's ionosphere and upper atmosphere, creating geomagnetic storms and aurora.

37. D: In 1912, Alfred Wegener proposed that the continents once formed a single land mass called Pangaea, but have since drifted apart. Theories about the Earth's magnetic fields and plate tectonics did not emerge until years later. Once they did, they helped produce evidence to support Wegener's theory.

38. B: The Richter scale determines the magnitude of an earthquake by measuring the amount of seismic energy it releases. The formula used to calculate an earthquake's Richter magnitude takes the logarithm of the horizontal amplitude of the earthquake's seismic waves into account, and also makes adjustments for the position of the seismograph relative to the earthquake.

39. A: An earthquake with a Richter magnitude of 1.5 will probably not be felt, and will not cause any damage. Earthquakes with magnitudes of less than 2.0 are usually not felt, and those with magnitudes of less than 5.0 typically do not seriously damage well-constructed buildings. Earthquakes with magnitudes of 6.0 or greater can cause damage to even well-constructed buildings.

40. B: The process that causes lithospheric plates to move over the surface of the mantle is called convection. The liquid in the lower portion of the mantle is heated by the Earth's core and rises to the surface, pushing aside cooler liquid that is already there. This liquid cools, and is in turn pushed aside by hotter liquid that has risen from below. This cycle, called convection, creates constant movement in the mantle that contributes to the motion of the tectonic plates.

41. D: Water in the liquid state generally has a higher density than water in the solid state (ice). Unlike most other substances, which become progressively denser as they grow colder, water's density only increases until it reaches a maximum density around 4 °C, after which it begins to decrease as the temperature drops further.

42. B: The fact that water's specific heat capacity is second only to that of ammonia means that it takes more energy to increase the temperature of ammonia than it does to increase the temperature of water. Specific heat capacity refers to the amount of energy required to increase the

temperature of a substance by one degree Celsius. Ammonia has the highest specific heat capacity of all substances, and the specific heat capacity of water is the second highest.

43. B: Water that evaporates from oceans can precipitate over land due to the process of advection. Water vapor is less dense than air, and this difference in density produces convection currents that move the vapor, allowing it to condense and precipitate over land masses.

44. D: Water is likely to have the shortest residence time in the atmosphere. Water molecules linger in the atmosphere for an estimated 9 days, while their residence time in glaciers may range from 20 to 100 years. Water molecules reside in lakes for approximately 50 to 100 years, and they stay in rivers for two to six months.

45. C: When water changes directly from a solid to a gas, skipping the liquid state, it is known as sublimation. It typically occurs when snow or ice is exposed to direct sunlight, and it is possible at unusually low atmospheric pressure points.

46. C: The main manmade cause of "dead zones" in portions of oceans and lakes that normally host abundant aquatic life is the use of chemical fertilizers. These fertilizers, which are high in nitrogen and phosphorous, enter lakes and rivers in water runoff and become concentrated in certain areas. This concentration, called eutrophication, eventually depletes the water's oxygen levels and renders it incapable of supporting life.

47. C: The majority of the solar energy that reaches Earth is absorbed by the oceans, which make up 71 percent of the Earth's surface. Because of water's high specific heat capacity, oceans can absorb and store large quantities of heat, thus preventing drastic increases in the overall atmospheric temperature.

48. A: The majority of weather phenomena occur in the Earth's troposphere. The troposphere is comprised of the area roughly 8-15 kilometers above the Earth's surface. It contains the majority of the mass of Earth's atmosphere and 99 percent of its water vapor.

49. A: According to the Köppen Climate Classification System, regions with continental climates are most commonly found in the interior regions of large landmasses. The continental climate is characterized by low levels of precipitation and large seasonal temperature variations.

50. C: Tropical climate zones are characterized by frequent rainfall, especially during the monsoon season, and by moderate temperatures that vary little from season to season or between night and day. Tropical zones do experience frequent rainfall, which leads to abundant vegetation.

51. D: It is true that the ocean's salinity is usually between 34 and 35 parts per thousand, or 200 parts per million. Oceans comprise about 70.8 percent of the Earth's surface, and the ocean's deepest point is over 10,000 meters below sea level. The Mediterranean is considered a sea, not an ocean.

52. B: A guyot is defined as a seamount with a flattened top. The term "seamount" refers to any undersea volcano that is more than 1,000 meters tall. Undersea troughs are called trenches, and undersea mountain chains are called mid-ocean ridges.

53. B: Approximately 96.5 percent of seawater is comprised of hydrogen and oxygen. Although seawater does contain sodium, chlorine, magnesium, sulfur, and other dissolved solids, its primary components are the same substances that make up fresh water.

54. C: It is true that subsurface currents are driven by temperature and density variations, while surface currents are driven by wind. Ocean currents affect vast quantities of seawater and strongly influence the climate of Earth's landmasses.

55. A: The appearance of the Coriolis effect in the Earth's oceans is caused by the Earth's rotation. The Coriolis effect results when free objects such as water move over a rotating surface such as the Earth. As water moves from the poles towards the Equator, it curves slightly westward, while water moving in the opposite direction (from the Equator towards the poles) moves slightly eastward.

56. C: The Gulf Stream, which is a surface current that originates in the Gulf of Mexico and travels across the Atlantic Ocean, makes the climate of Northern Europe warmer. After traveling up the eastern coast of the U.S., the Gulf Stream splits into two forks. The North Atlantic Drift travels across the ocean to warm Europe, while the southern fork travels toward West Africa.

57. C: Thermohaline circulation is caused by variations in seawater density caused by both temperature and salinity differences. This process, which affects subsurface ocean currents, contributes to the mixing of seawater and accounts for the relative uniformity of the water's physical and chemical properties.

58. C: When cold, nutrient-rich water is allowed to rise to the surface because winds parallel to a landmass's coast blow the surface water towards the open sea, it is called upwelling. Upwelling brings the remains of dead sea creatures to the surface, providing food for phytoplankton. Zooplanktons consume the phytoplankton, and larger organisms consume the zooplanktons. Thus, upwelling allows marine life to thrive near coastal areas.

59. D: The frequency of ocean waves is measured by the number of wave crests that pass a given point each second. The crest of a wave is its highest point, and the trough is its lowest point. The distance between two subsequent crests is called wavelength, and the height is the distance between a single wave's trough and crest.

60. B: When the accumulation of snow and ice exceeds ablation, a glacier will gradually form. Ablation is the sloughing off of ice and snow through melting, evaporation, sublimation, and wind erosion. When snow and ice accumulate faster than ablation occurs, a glacier will form and continue to gain mass until the rate of ablation overtakes the rate of accumulation.

61. D: The Cretaceous-Tertiary event, during which non-avian dinosaurs became extinct, occurred approximately 65.5 million years ago during the Mesozoic era. It is the most recent of the five major extinction events that have occurred throughout the Earth's history.

62. B: Stratigraphic dating is not a radiometric dating process because it does not consider the radioactive properties of materials to estimate their dates. Instead, it relies on the Law of Superposition to estimate relative ages by comparing the relative depths of materials.

63. C: In the field of geology, the term "uniformitarianism" refers to the belief that the natural forces, laws, and processes that shape the Earth have remained relatively constant over geologic time. This belief contradicts catastrophism, which maintains that dramatic events have been the primary forces involved in shaping the Earth.

64. D: The field of stratigraphy is divided into several subfields, each of which focuses on a unique aspect of sedimentary material and yields unique insights about the material's age. In the subfield of chronostratigraphy, a material's age is estimated by determining when it was formed or deposited. The study of the vertical layering of rock types is called lithostratigraphy, and the study

of fossil ages in rock layers is called biostratigraphy. Magnetostratigraphy examines data about changes in detrital remanent magnetism (DRM) at the time rocks were formed.

65. A: A fossil that is 37 million years old is an example of an absolute age. Absolute dating, which can be accomplished through the use of radiometric techniques, establishes precise ages for materials, while stratigraphic techniques only produce relative dates. Relative dating can pinpoint approximate ages for rocks and fossils based on clues in the surrounding rock, but it cannot be used to determine absolute age.

66. C: In geochronology, an eon is the longest time period, lasting at least half a billion years. An era lasts several hundred million years, an epoch measures tens of millions of years, and an age is shorter than 10 million years but longer than one million years.

67. C: The Mesozoic era is comprised of the Triassic, Jurassic, and Cretaceous periods. It was preceded by the Paleozoic era, of which the Permian is the last period. The Triassic period ended about 200 million years ago, and was followed by the Jurassic period. The Jurassic period gave way to the Cretaceous period just under 150 million years ago.

68. C: In his 1924 work, *The Origin of Life*, Alexander Oparin argued that life arose on Earth through a "primordial soup" that is no longer possible because of atmospheric oxygen.

69. C: According to current theories, the Earth was formed approximately 4.5 billion years ago. This date has been established through the use of radiometric dating performed on meteorite fossils.

70. B: The most severe mass extinction event in Earth's history was the Permian-Triassic Event. It occurred approximately 251.4 million years ago, and resulted in the extinction of 96 percent of all marine species and 70 percent of terrestrial vertebrate species.

71. C: Prokaryotes, or simple cells that lack a nucleus, appeared on Earth approximately 3.8 billion years ago. Eukaryotes, or complex cells, emerged 2 billion years ago, and arthropods developed about 570 million years ago. Amphibians emerged approximately 360 million years ago.

72. D: The Cambrian Explosion is best described as the dramatic increase in biodiversity that began about 530 million years ago and resulted in the emergence of complex animals over a period of millions of years. Evidence for this "explosion" of life comes mainly from fossil records. There are many possible explanations for it, ranging from an increase in oxygen levels to the development of eyes.

73. D: Expansion in the redshifts of galaxies, measurements of cosmic microwave background radiation, and measurements of the distribution of quasars and galaxies are all considered observational evidence in support of the Big Bang Theory. The abundance of certain "primordial elements" is also consistent with the theory.

74. C: The Cosmological Principle is best described as a working assumption that has testable structural consequences. The principle, which underlies existing cosmological theories, assumes that the view of the universe possessed by observers on Earth is not distorted by their observational location. The observable implications of this theory are homogeneity (the same types of observational evidence are available regardless of one's vantage point within the universe) and isotropy (the same observational evidence is available by looking in any given direction from a single vantage point).

75. A: Redshift is observed when a light-emitting object moves away from an observer. The observation of cosmological redshift supports the notion that the universe is expanding and the distance between Earth and far away galaxies is increasing. Redshift is an increase in the wavelength of light that appears visually as a movement toward the "red" end of the spectrum.

76. D: The physical structure of the universe is thought to consist of filaments (walls of superclusters, clusters, and galaxies) that surround large, bubble-like voids. Filaments are the largest structures in the universe, with some forming huge structures like the Great Wall and the Sloan Great Wall.

77. B: It is true that galaxies are gravitationally bound so that structures within them orbit around the center. Galaxies do contain dark matter, and only the largest "giant" galaxies contain over one trillion stars. The smallest "dwarf" galaxies contain as few as 10 million stars. Clusters and superclusters are comprised of many galaxies.

78. A: The structure of the Milky Way galaxy is spiral, meaning it has curved "arms" stretching out from a central point. While spiral galaxies have a flat, disc-like appearance, elliptical galaxies are three-dimensional and appear to be roughly the same shape regardless of the viewing angle.

79. A: The Hertzsprung-Russell (H-R) Diagram is used primarily to determine a star's age by comparing its temperature and luminosity. These two variables are plotted, and a given star's values can be compared to those of other stars to estimate its age and evolutionary stage. Stars on the Main Sequence of the diagram have roughly proportional luminosity and temperature values, while white dwarf stars have low luminosity relative to their temperature. Some giant stars have low temperatures relative to their luminosity.

80. A: The distance from the Earth to the Sun is equal to one astronomical unit. An astronomical unit (AU) is equal to 93 million miles, and is far smaller than a light year or a parsec. A light year is defined as the distance light can travel in a vacuum in one year, and is equal to roughly 64,341 AU. A parsec is the parallax of one arcsecond, and is equal to 206.26×10^3 astronomical units.

81. B: The energy radiated by stars is produced by nuclear fusion. This is the process whereby the nuclei of individual atoms bind together to form heavier elements and release energy outward. By the time this energy, which is created in the star's core, reaches the outer walls of the star, it exists in the form of light.

82. A: The stream of charged particles that escape the Sun's gravitational pull is called solar wind. Solar wind is comprised primarily of protons and electrons, and these particles are deflected away from the Earth by its magnetic field. When stray particles do manage to enter the atmosphere, they cause the aurorae (Northern and Southern Lights) and geomagnetic storms that can affect power grids.

83. C: Venus is not a gas giant. The four gas giants are Jupiter, Saturn, Uranus, and Neptune. While these "gas giants" are larger than Earth and are comprised mostly of gases, Venus is a terrestrial planet that is comparable in size to the Earth.

84. D: The asteroid belt in our solar system is located between Mars and Jupiter. The asteroid belt is populated by asteroids and dwarf planets that are distributed thinly enough that spacecraft can pass though the belt with relative ease.

85. D: Gravitational collapse and high-energy collisions are both proposed explanations for the formation of black holes. Gravitational collapse occurs when the outward pressure exerted by an

object is too weak to resist that object's own gravity. Collisions that produce conditions of sufficient density could also, in theory, create black holes. The accretion of matter is considered observational evidence for the existence of black holes.

86. B: A total solar eclipse can be observed only by viewers located within the umbra. The umbra is the darkest part of the shadow, and the light source is not visible from it. The penumbra is the lighter portion of the shadow from which the light source is partially visible. In a solar eclipse, the Moon passes between the Earth and the Sun, and viewers in the umbra experience a total solar eclipse.
I. Basic Scientific Principles of Earth and Space Sciences

87. C: The atomic number of an element is defined by the total number of protons it contains, and elements are arranged on the periodic table by atomic number. The atomic mass of an element is the sum total of its protons and neutrons.

88. B: The main distinction between the isotopes carbon-12 and carbon-13 is that they have different mass numbers. Isotopes of a given element all have the same atomic number, since atomic number (also known as proton number) is the defining characteristic of each element. However, they have different neutron numbers, which causes them to have varying mass numbers as well. Both carbon-12 and carbon-13 are stable isotopes, meaning they do not experience observable radioactive decay.

89. D: Electrons are elementary particles with no known components, so it is not true that they have a nucleus. Electrons are negatively charged, and they are arranged in levels. Electrons gravitate toward the lowest energy level possible, and they have very little mass (roughly 1/1836 of the mass of a proton).

90. A: Chemical compounds are formed when valence electrons from atoms of two different elements are shared or transferred. Valence electrons are the electrons located in the outermost shell of the atom, and they occupy the highest energy level. Atoms may form compounds by sharing valence electrons (covalent bonding) or by transferring electrons.

91. C: The state of matter in which atoms have the strongest bond is the solid state. Matter, which is defined as any substance that has mass and occupies space, can exist as a solid, liquid, gas, or plasma. The atoms or molecules that form solids possess the strongest bonds, while those that form plasma possess the weakest bonds.

92. B: A closed thermodynamic system can exchange heat and work, but not matter, with its surrounding environment. In contrast, an isolated system cannot exchange heat, work, or matter with its surrounding environment, so its mass and energy levels always remain constant. Open systems can exchange heat, work, and mass with their surrounding environments.

93. A: The formula for calculating kinetic energy is $\frac{1}{2} mv^2$, where m=mass and v=velocity. Kinetic energy is defined as the energy of an object in motion. Potential energy, or stored energy, is measured using the formula mgh, where m=mass, g=gravity, and h=height.

94. B: The first law of classical thermodynamics states that energy can neither be created nor destroyed. The zeroth law is concerned with thermodynamic equilibrium, and the second and third laws discuss entropy.

95. C: James Hutton is best known for proposing the theory of uniformitarianism. This geological theory, which is essentially the opposite of catastrophism, suggests that the laws and forces acting on the Earth have remained basically the same since the beginning of geologic time.

96. A: The correct formula for converting Fahrenheit measurements to Celsius measurements is 5/9 (F – 32), where F is the temperature in Fahrenheit.

97. A: A calorimeter is used to measure changes in heat. This instrument uses a thermometer to measure the amount of energy necessary to increase the temperature of water.

98. A: Commercial nuclear reactors generate electricity through the process of nuclear fission. The fission process is used to heat water, which in turn generates steam that is used to produce electricity. This process is controlled to ensure safety, but it does produce nuclear waste that requires the use of extensive procedures to dispose of it safely.

99. C: The results of the regression analysis show that there is a weak positive correlation between the two variables, as evidenced by the fact that data points with higher values for the independent variable (x-axis) also have higher corresponding values for the dependent variable (y-axis). However, correlation does not equal causation, and it cannot be established that a change in the independent variable causes a corresponding change in the dependent variable without additional information.

100. B: Random error could be caused by extraneous disturbances that cannot be controlled. Random error is that which does not affect experimental results in a consistent, patterned way. In contrast, systematic error affects all experimental results consistently. For example, if an instrument is calibrated improperly, all experimental results will be skewed in the same direction.

How to Overcome Test Anxiety

Just the thought of taking a test is enough to make most people a little nervous. A test is an important event that can have a long-term impact on your future, so it's important to take it seriously and it's natural to feel anxious about performing well. But just because anxiety is normal, that doesn't mean that it's helpful in test taking, or that you should simply accept it as part of your life. Anxiety can have a variety of effects. These effects can be mild, like making you feel slightly nervous, or severe, like blocking your ability to focus or remember even a simple detail.

If you experience test anxiety—whether severe or mild—it's important to know how to beat it. To discover this, first you need to understand what causes test anxiety.

Causes of Test Anxiety

While we often think of anxiety as an uncontrollable emotional state, it can actually be caused by simple, practical things. One of the most common causes of test anxiety is that a person does not feel adequately prepared for their test. This feeling can be the result of many different issues such as poor study habits or lack of organization, but the most common culprit is time management. Starting to study too late, failing to organize your study time to cover all of the material, or being distracted while you study will mean that you're not well prepared for the test. This may lead to cramming the night before, which will cause you to be physically and mentally exhausted for the test. Poor time management also contributes to feelings of stress, fear, and hopelessness as you realize you are not well prepared but don't know what to do about it.

Other times, test anxiety is not related to your preparation for the test but comes from unresolved fear. This may be a past failure on a test, or poor performance on tests in general. It may come from comparing yourself to others who seem to be performing better or from the stress of living up to expectations. Anxiety may be driven by fears of the future—how failure on this test would affect your educational and career goals. These fears are often completely irrational, but they can still negatively impact your test performance.

Review Video: 3 Reasons You Have Test Anxiety
Visit mometrix.com/academy and enter code: 428468

Elements of Test Anxiety

As mentioned earlier, test anxiety is considered to be an emotional state, but it has physical and mental components as well. Sometimes you may not even realize that you are suffering from test anxiety until you notice the physical symptoms. These can include trembling hands, rapid heartbeat, sweating, nausea, and tense muscles. Extreme anxiety may lead to fainting or vomiting. Obviously, any of these symptoms can have a negative impact on testing. It is important to recognize them as soon as they begin to occur so that you can address the problem before it damages your performance.

Review Video: 3 Ways to Tell You Have Test Anxiety
Visit mometrix.com/academy and enter code: 927847

The mental components of test anxiety include trouble focusing and inability to remember learned information. During a test, your mind is on high alert, which can help you recall information and stay focused for an extended period of time. However, anxiety interferes with your mind's natural processes, causing you to blank out, even on the questions you know well. The strain of testing during anxiety makes it difficult to stay focused, especially on a test that may take several hours. Extreme anxiety can take a huge mental toll, making it difficult not only to recall test information but even to understand the test questions or pull your thoughts together.

Review Video: How Test Anxiety Affects Memory
Visit mometrix.com/academy and enter code: 609003

Effects of Test Anxiety

Test anxiety is like a disease—if left untreated, it will get progressively worse. Anxiety leads to poor performance, and this reinforces the feelings of fear and failure, which in turn lead to poor performances on subsequent tests. It can grow from a mild nervousness to a crippling condition. If allowed to progress, test anxiety can have a big impact on your schooling, and consequently on your future.

Test anxiety can spread to other parts of your life. Anxiety on tests can become anxiety in any stressful situation, and blanking on a test can turn into panicking in a job situation. But fortunately, you don't have to let anxiety rule your testing and determine your grades. There are a number of relatively simple steps you can take to move past anxiety and function normally on a test and in the rest of life.

Review Video: How Test Anxiety Impacts Your Grades
Visit mometrix.com/academy and enter code: 939819

Physical Steps for Beating Test Anxiety

While test anxiety is a serious problem, the good news is that it can be overcome. It doesn't have to control your ability to think and remember information. While it may take time, you can begin taking steps today to beat anxiety.

Just as your first hint that you may be struggling with anxiety comes from the physical symptoms, the first step to treating it is also physical. Rest is crucial for having a clear, strong mind. If you are tired, it is much easier to give in to anxiety. But if you establish good sleep habits, your body and mind will be ready to perform optimally, without the strain of exhaustion. Additionally, sleeping well helps you to retain information better, so you're more likely to recall the answers when you see the test questions.

Getting good sleep means more than going to bed on time. It's important to allow your brain time to relax. Take study breaks from time to time so it doesn't get overworked, and don't study right before bed. Take time to rest your mind before trying to rest your body, or you may find it difficult to fall asleep.

Review Video: The Importance of Sleep for Your Brain
Visit mometrix.com/academy and enter code: 319338

Along with sleep, other aspects of physical health are important in preparing for a test. Good nutrition is vital for good brain function. Sugary foods and drinks may give a burst of energy but this burst is followed by a crash, both physically and emotionally. Instead, fuel your body with protein and vitamin-rich foods.

Also, drink plenty of water. Dehydration can lead to headaches and exhaustion, especially if your brain is already under stress from the rigors of the test. Particularly if your test is a long one, drink water during the breaks. And if possible, take an energy-boosting snack to eat between sections.

Review Video: How Diet Can Affect your Mood
Visit mometrix.com/academy and enter code: 624317

Along with sleep and diet, a third important part of physical health is exercise. Maintaining a steady workout schedule is helpful, but even taking 5-minute study breaks to walk can help get your blood pumping faster and clear your head. Exercise also releases endorphins, which contribute to a positive feeling and can help combat test anxiety.

When you nurture your physical health, you are also contributing to your mental health. If your body is healthy, your mind is much more likely to be healthy as well. So take time to rest, nourish your body with healthy food and water, and get moving as much as possible. Taking these physical steps will make you stronger and more able to take the mental steps necessary to overcome test anxiety.

Review Video: How to Stay Healthy and Prevent Test Anxiety
Visit mometrix.com/academy and enter code: 877894

Mental Steps for Beating Test Anxiety

Working on the mental side of test anxiety can be more challenging, but as with the physical side, there are clear steps you can take to overcome it. As mentioned earlier, test anxiety often stems from lack of preparation, so the obvious solution is to prepare for the test. Effective studying may be the most important weapon you have for beating test anxiety, but you can and should employ several other mental tools to combat fear.

First, boost your confidence by reminding yourself of past success—tests or projects that you aced. If you're putting as much effort into preparing for this test as you did for those, there's no reason you should expect to fail here. Work hard to prepare; then trust your preparation.

Second, surround yourself with encouraging people. It can be helpful to find a study group, but be sure that the people you're around will encourage a positive attitude. If you spend time with others who are anxious or cynical, this will only contribute to your own anxiety. Look for others who are motivated to study hard from a desire to succeed, not from a fear of failure.

Third, reward yourself. A test is physically and mentally tiring, even without anxiety, and it can be helpful to have something to look forward to. Plan an activity following the test, regardless of the outcome, such as going to a movie or getting ice cream.

When you are taking the test, if you find yourself beginning to feel anxious, remind yourself that you know the material. Visualize successfully completing the test. Then take a few deep, relaxing breaths and return to it. Work through the questions carefully but with confidence, knowing that you are capable of succeeding.

Developing a healthy mental approach to test taking will also aid in other areas of life. Test anxiety affects more than just the actual test—it can be damaging to your mental health and even contribute to depression. It's important to beat test anxiety before it becomes a problem for more than testing.

Review Video: Test Anxiety and Depression
Visit mometrix.com/academy and enter code: 904704

Study Strategy

Being prepared for the test is necessary to combat anxiety, but what does being prepared look like? You may study for hours on end and still not feel prepared. What you need is a strategy for test prep. The next few pages outline our recommended steps to help you plan out and conquer the challenge of preparation.

Step 1: Scope Out the Test

Learn everything you can about the format (multiple choice, essay, etc.) and what will be on the test. Gather any study materials, course outlines, or sample exams that may be available. Not only will this help you to prepare, but knowing what to expect can help to alleviate test anxiety.

Step 2: Map Out the Material

Look through the textbook or study guide and make note of how many chapters or sections it has. Then divide these over the time you have. For example, if a book has 15 chapters and you have five days to study, you need to cover three chapters each day. Even better, if you have the time, leave an extra day at the end for overall review after you have gone through the material in depth.

If time is limited, you may need to prioritize the material. Look through it and make note of which sections you think you already have a good grasp on, and which need review. While you are studying, skim quickly through the familiar sections and take more time on the challenging parts. Write out your plan so you don't get lost as you go. Having a written plan also helps you feel more in control of the study, so anxiety is less likely to arise from feeling overwhelmed at the amount to cover. A sample plan may look like this:

- Day 1: Skim chapters 1–4, study chapter 5 (especially pages 31–33)
- Day 2: Study chapters 6–7, skim chapters 8–9
- Day 3: Skim chapter 10, study chapters 11–12 (especially pages 87–90)
- Day 4: Study chapters 13–15
- Day 5: Overall review (focus most on chapters 5, 6, and 12), take practice test

Step 3: Gather Your Tools

Decide what study method works best for you. Do you prefer to highlight in the book as you study and then go back over the highlighted portions? Or do you type out notes of the important information? Or is it helpful to make flashcards that you can carry with you? Assemble the pens, index cards, highlighters, post-it notes, and any other materials you may need so you won't be distracted by getting up to find things while you study.

If you're having a hard time retaining the information or organizing your notes, experiment with different methods. For example, try color-coding by subject with colored pens, highlighters, or post-it notes. If you learn better by hearing, try recording yourself reading your notes so you can listen while in the car, working out, or simply sitting at your desk. Ask a friend to quiz you from your flashcards, or try teaching someone the material to solidify it in your mind.

Step 4: Create Your Environment

It's important to avoid distractions while you study. This includes both the obvious distractions like visitors and the subtle distractions like an uncomfortable chair (or a too-comfortable couch that makes you want to fall asleep). Set up the best study environment possible: good lighting and a comfortable work area. If background music helps you focus, you may want to turn it on, but otherwise keep the room quiet. If you are using a computer to take notes, be sure you don't have any other windows open, especially applications like social media, games, or anything else that could distract you. Silence your phone and turn off notifications. Be sure to keep water close by so you stay hydrated while you study (but avoid unhealthy drinks and snacks).

Also, take into account the best time of day to study. Are you freshest first thing in the morning? Try to set aside some time then to work through the material. Is your mind clearer in the afternoon or evening? Schedule your study session then. Another method is to study at the same time of day that you will take the test, so that your brain gets used to working on the material at that time and will be ready to focus at test time.

Step 5: Study!

Once you have done all the study preparation, it's time to settle into the actual studying. Sit down, take a few moments to settle your mind so you can focus, and begin to follow your study plan. Don't give in to distractions or let yourself procrastinate. This is your time to prepare so you'll be ready to fearlessly approach the test. Make the most of the time and stay focused.

Of course, you don't want to burn out. If you study too long you may find that you're not retaining the information very well. Take regular study breaks. For example, taking five minutes out of every hour to walk briskly, breathing deeply and swinging your arms, can help your mind stay fresh.

As you get to the end of each chapter or section, it's a good idea to do a quick review. Remind yourself of what you learned and work on any difficult parts. When you feel that you've mastered the material, move on to the next part. At the end of your study session, briefly skim through your notes again.

But while review is helpful, cramming last minute is NOT. If at all possible, work ahead so that you won't need to fit all your study into the last day. Cramming overloads your brain with more information than it can process and retain, and your tired mind may struggle to recall even previously learned information when it is overwhelmed with last-minute study. Also, the urgent nature of cramming and the stress placed on your brain contribute to anxiety. You'll be more likely to go to the test feeling unprepared and having trouble thinking clearly.

So don't cram, and don't stay up late before the test, even just to review your notes at a leisurely pace. Your brain needs rest more than it needs to go over the information again. In fact, plan to finish your studies by noon or early afternoon the day before the test. Give your brain the rest of the day to relax or focus on other things, and get a good night's sleep. Then you will be fresh for the test and better able to recall what you've studied.

Step 6: Take a practice test

Many courses offer sample tests, either online or in the study materials. This is an excellent resource to check whether you have mastered the material, as well as to prepare for the test format and environment.

Check the test format ahead of time: the number of questions, the type (multiple choice, free response, etc.), and the time limit. Then create a plan for working through them. For example, if you have 30 minutes to take a 60-question test, your limit is 30 seconds per question. Spend less time on the questions you know well so that you can take more time on the difficult ones.

If you have time to take several practice tests, take the first one open book, with no time limit. Work through the questions at your own pace and make sure you fully understand them. Gradually work up to taking a test under test conditions: sit at a desk with all study materials put away and set a timer. Pace yourself to make sure you finish the test with time to spare and go back to check your answers if you have time.

After each test, check your answers. On the questions you missed, be sure you understand why you missed them. Did you misread the question (tests can use tricky wording)? Did you forget the information? Or was it something you hadn't learned? Go back and study any shaky areas that the practice tests reveal.

Taking these tests not only helps with your grade, but also aids in combating test anxiety. If you're already used to the test conditions, you're less likely to worry about it, and working through tests until you're scoring well gives you a confidence boost. Go through the practice tests until you feel comfortable, and then you can go into the test knowing that you're ready for it.

Test Tips

On test day, you should be confident, knowing that you've prepared well and are ready to answer the questions. But aside from preparation, there are several test day strategies you can employ to maximize your performance.

First, as stated before, get a good night's sleep the night before the test (and for several nights before that, if possible). Go into the test with a fresh, alert mind rather than staying up late to study.

Try not to change too much about your normal routine on the day of the test. It's important to eat a nutritious breakfast, but if you normally don't eat breakfast at all, consider eating just a protein bar. If you're a coffee drinker, go ahead and have your normal coffee. Just make sure you time it so that the caffeine doesn't wear off right in the middle of your test. Avoid sugary beverages, and drink enough water to stay hydrated but not so much that you need a restroom break 10 minutes into the test. If your test isn't first thing in the morning, consider going for a walk or doing a light workout before the test to get your blood flowing.

Allow yourself enough time to get ready, and leave for the test with plenty of time to spare so you won't have the anxiety of scrambling to arrive in time. Another reason to be early is to select a good seat. It's helpful to sit away from doors and windows, which can be distracting. Find a good seat, get out your supplies, and settle your mind before the test begins.

When the test begins, start by going over the instructions carefully, even if you already know what to expect. Make sure you avoid any careless mistakes by following the directions.

Then begin working through the questions, pacing yourself as you've practiced. If you're not sure on an answer, don't spend too much time on it, and don't let it shake your confidence. Either skip it and come back later, or eliminate as many wrong answers as possible and guess among the remaining ones. Don't dwell on these questions as you continue—put them out of your mind and focus on what lies ahead.

Be sure to read all of the answer choices, even if you're sure the first one is the right answer. Sometimes you'll find a better one if you keep reading. But don't second-guess yourself if you do immediately know the answer. Your gut instinct is usually right. Don't let test anxiety rob you of the information you know.

If you have time at the end of the test (and if the test format allows), go back and review your answers. Be cautious about changing any, since your first instinct tends to be correct, but make sure you didn't misread any of the questions or accidentally mark the wrong answer choice. Look over any you skipped and make an educated guess.

At the end, leave the test feeling confident. You've done your best, so don't waste time worrying about your performance or wishing you could change anything. Instead, celebrate the successful completion of this test. And finally, use this test to learn how to deal with anxiety even better next time.

Review Video: 5 Tips to Beat Test Anxiety
Visit mometrix.com/academy and enter code: 570656

Important Qualification

Not all anxiety is created equal. If your test anxiety is causing major issues in your life beyond the classroom or testing center, or if you are experiencing troubling physical symptoms related to your anxiety, it may be a sign of a serious physiological or psychological condition. If this sounds like your situation, we strongly encourage you to seek professional help.

How to Overcome Your Fear of Math

The word *math* is enough to strike fear into most hearts. How many of us have memories of sitting through confusing lectures, wrestling over mind-numbing homework, or taking tests that still seem incomprehensible even after hours of study? Years after graduation, many still shudder at these memories.

The fact is, math is not just a classroom subject. It has real-world implications that you face every day, whether you realize it or not. This may be balancing your monthly budget, deciding how many supplies to buy for a project, or simply splitting a meal check with friends. The idea of daily confrontations with math can be so paralyzing that some develop a condition known as *math anxiety*.

But you do NOT need to be paralyzed by this anxiety! In fact, while you may have thought all your life that you're not good at math, or that your brain isn't wired to understand it, the truth is that you may have been conditioned to think this way. From your earliest school days, the way you were taught affected the way you viewed different subjects. And the way math has been taught has changed.

Several decades ago, there was a shift in American math classrooms. The focus changed from traditional problem-solving to a conceptual view of topics, de-emphasizing the importance of learning the basics and building on them. The solid foundation necessary for math progression and confidence was undermined. Math became more of a vague concept than a concrete idea. Today, it is common to think of math, not as a straightforward system, but as a mysterious, complicated method that can't be fully understood unless you're a genius.

This is why you may still have nightmares about being called on to answer a difficult problem in front of the class. Math anxiety is a very real, though unnecessary, fear.

Math anxiety may begin with a single class period. Let's say you missed a day in 6th grade math and never quite understood the concept that was taught while you were gone. Since math is cumulative, with each new concept building on past ones, this could very well affect the rest of your math career. Without that one day's knowledge, it will be difficult to understand any other concepts that link to it. Rather than realizing that you're just missing one key piece, you may begin to believe that you're simply not capable of understanding math.

This belief can change the way you approach other classes, career options, and everyday life experiences, if you become anxious at the thought that math might be required. A student who loves science may choose a different path of study upon realizing that multiple math classes will be required for a degree. An aspiring medical student may hesitate at the thought of going through the necessary math classes. For some this anxiety escalates into a more extreme state known as *math phobia*.

Math anxiety is challenging to address because it is rooted deeply and may come from a variety of causes: an embarrassing moment in class, a teacher who did not explain concepts well and contributed to a shaky foundation, or a failed test that contributed to the belief of math failure.

These causes add up over time, encouraged by society's popular view that math is hard and unpleasant. Eventually a person comes to firmly believe that he or she is simply bad at math. This belief makes it difficult to grasp new concepts or even remember old ones. Homework and test grades begin to slip, which only confirms the belief. The poor performance is not due to lack of ability but is caused by math anxiety.

Math anxiety is an emotional issue, not a lack of intelligence. But when it becomes deeply rooted, it can become more than just an emotional problem. Physical symptoms appear. Blood pressure may rise and heartbeat may quicken at the sight of a math problem – or even the thought of math! This fear leads to a mental block. When someone with math anxiety is asked to perform a calculation, even a basic problem can seem overwhelming and impossible. The emotional and physical response to the thought of math prevents the brain from working through it logically.

The more this happens, the more a person's confidence drops, and the more math anxiety is generated. This vicious cycle must be broken!

The first step in breaking the cycle is to go back to very beginning and make sure you really understand the basics of how math works and why it works. It is not enough to memorize rules for multiplication and division. If you don't know WHY these rules work, your foundation will be shaky and you will be at risk of developing a phobia. Understanding mathematical concepts not only promotes confidence and security, but allows you to build on this understanding for new concepts. Additionally, you can solve unfamiliar problems using familiar concepts and processes.

Why is it that students in other countries regularly outperform American students in math? The answer likely boils down to a couple of things: the foundation of mathematical conceptual understanding and societal perception. While students in the US are not expected to *like* or *get* math, in many other nations, students are expected not only to understand math but also to excel at it.

Changing the American view of math that leads to math anxiety is a monumental task. It requires changing the training of teachers nationwide, from kindergarten through high school, so that they learn to teach the *why* behind math and to combat the wrong math views that students may develop. It also involves changing the stigma associated with math, so that it is no longer viewed as unpleasant and incomprehensible. While these are necessary changes, they are challenging and will take time. But in the meantime, math anxiety is not irreversible—it can be faced and defeated, one person at a time.

False Beliefs

One reason math anxiety has taken such hold is that several false beliefs have been created and shared until they became widely accepted. Some of these unhelpful beliefs include the following:

There is only one way to solve a math problem. In the same way that you can choose from different driving routes and still arrive at the same house, you can solve a math problem using different methods and still find the correct answer. A person who understands the reasoning behind math calculations may be able to look at an unfamiliar concept and find the right answer, just by applying logic to the knowledge they already have. This approach may be different than what is taught in the classroom, but it is still valid. Unfortunately, even many teachers view math as a subject where the best course of action is to memorize the rule or process for each problem rather than as a place for students to exercise logic and creativity in finding a solution.

Many people don't have a mind for math. A person who has struggled due to poor teaching or math anxiety may falsely believe that he or she doesn't have the mental capacity to grasp mathematical concepts. Most of the time, this is false. Many people find that when they are relieved of their math anxiety, they have more than enough brainpower to understand math.

Men are naturally better at math than women. Even though research has shown this to be false, many young women still avoid math careers and classes because of their belief that their math abilities are inferior. Many girls have come to believe that math is a male skill and have given up trying to understand or enjoy it.

Counting aids are bad. Something like counting on your fingers or drawing out a problem to visualize it may be frowned on as childish or a crutch, but these devices can help you get a tangible understanding of a problem or a concept.

Sadly, many students buy into these ideologies at an early age. A young girl who enjoys math class may be conditioned to think that she doesn't actually have the brain for it because math is for boys, and may turn her energies to other pursuits, permanently closing the door on a wide range of opportunities. A child who finds the right answer but doesn't follow the teacher's method may believe that he is doing it wrong and isn't good at math. A student who never had a problem with math before may have a poor teacher and become confused, yet believe that the problem is because she doesn't have a mathematical mind.

Students who have bought into these erroneous beliefs quickly begin to add their own anxieties, adapting them to their own personal situations:

I'll never use this in real life. A huge number of people wrongly believe that math is irrelevant outside the classroom. By adopting this mindset, they are handicapping themselves for a life in a mathematical world, as well as limiting their career choices. When they are inevitably faced with real-world math, they are conditioning themselves to respond with anxiety.

I'm not quick enough. While timed tests and quizzes, or even simply comparing yourself with other students in the class, can lead to this belief, speed is not an indicator of skill level. A person can work very slowly yet understand at a deep level.

If I can understand it, it's too easy. People with a low view of their own abilities tend to think that if they are able to grasp a concept, it must be simple. They cannot accept the idea that they are capable of understanding math. This belief will make it harder to learn, no matter how intelligent they are.

I just can't learn this. An overwhelming number of people think this, from young children to adults, and much of the time it is simply not true. But this mindset can turn into a self-fulfilling prophecy that keeps you from exercising and growing your math ability.

The good news is, each of these myths can be debunked. For most people, they are based on emotion and psychology, NOT on actual ability! It will take time, effort, and the desire to change, but change is possible. Even if you have spent years thinking that you don't have the capability to understand math, it is not too late to uncover your true ability and find relief from the anxiety that surrounds math.

Math Strategies

It is important to have a plan of attack to combat math anxiety. There are many useful strategies for pinpointing the fears or myths and eradicating them:

Go back to the basics. For most people, math anxiety stems from a poor foundation. You may think that you have a complete understanding of addition and subtraction, or even decimals and percentages, but make absolutely sure. Learning math is different from learning other subjects. For example, when you learn history, you study various time periods and places and events. It may be important to memorize dates or find out about the lives of famous people. When you move from US history to world history, there will be some overlap, but a large amount of the information will be new. Mathematical concepts, on the other hand, are very closely linked and highly dependent on each other. It's like climbing a ladder – if a rung is missing from your understanding, it may be difficult or impossible for you to climb any higher, no matter how hard you try. So go back and make sure your math foundation is strong. This may mean taking a remedial math course, going to a tutor to work through the shaky concepts, or just going through your old homework to make sure you really understand it.

Speak the language. Math has a large vocabulary of terms and phrases unique to working problems. Sometimes these are completely new terms, and sometimes they are common words, but are used differently in a math setting. If you can't speak the language, it will be very difficult to get a thorough understanding of the concepts. It's common for students to think that they don't understand math when they simply don't understand the vocabulary. The good news is that this is fairly easy to fix. Brushing up on any terms you aren't quite sure of can help bring the rest of the concepts into focus.

Check your anxiety level. When you think about math, do you feel nervous or uncomfortable? Do you struggle with feelings of inadequacy, even on concepts that you know you've already learned? It's important to understand your specific math anxieties, and what triggers them. When you catch yourself falling back on a false belief, mentally replace it with the truth. Don't let yourself believe that you can't learn, or that struggling with a concept means you'll never understand it. Instead, remind yourself of how much you've already learned and dwell on that past success. Visualize grasping the new concept, linking it to your old knowledge, and moving on to the next challenge. Also, learn how to manage anxiety when it arises. There are many techniques for coping with the irrational fears that rise to the surface when you enter the math classroom. This may include controlled breathing, replacing negative thoughts with positive ones, or visualizing success. Anxiety interferes with your ability to concentrate and absorb information, which in turn contributes to greater anxiety. If you can learn how to regain control of your thinking, you will be better able to pay attention, make progress, and succeed!

Don't go it alone. Like any deeply ingrained belief, math anxiety is not easy to eradicate. And there is no need for you to wrestle through it on your own. It will take time, and many people find that speaking with a counselor or psychiatrist helps. They can help you develop strategies for responding to anxiety and overcoming old ideas. Additionally, it can be very helpful to take a short course or seek out a math tutor to help you find and fix the missing rungs on your ladder and make sure that you're ready to progress to the next level. You can also find a number of math aids online: courses that will teach you mental devices for figuring out problems, how to get the most out of your math classes, etc.

Check your math attitude. No matter how much you want to learn and overcome your anxiety, you'll have trouble if you still have a negative attitude toward math. If you think it's too hard, or just have general feelings of dread about math, it will be hard to learn and to break through the anxiety. Work on cultivating a positive math attitude. Remind yourself that math is not just a hurdle to be cleared, but a valuable asset. When you view math with a positive attitude, you'll be much more likely to understand and even enjoy it. This is something you must do for yourself. You may find it helpful to visit with a counselor. Your tutor, friends, and family may cheer you on in your endeavors. But your greatest asset is yourself. You are inside your own mind – tell yourself what you need to hear. Relive past victories. Remind yourself that you are capable of understanding math. Root out any false beliefs that linger and replace them with positive truths. Even if it doesn't feel true at first, it will begin to affect your thinking and pave the way for a positive, anxiety-free mindset.

Aside from these general strategies, there are a number of specific practical things you can do to begin your journey toward overcoming math anxiety. Something as simple as learning a new note-taking strategy can change the way you approach math and give you more confidence and understanding. New study techniques can also make a huge difference.

Math anxiety leads to bad habits. If it causes you to be afraid of answering a question in class, you may gravitate toward the back row. You may be embarrassed to ask for help. And you may procrastinate on assignments, which leads to rushing through them at the last moment when it's too late to get a better understanding. It's important to identify your negative behaviors and replace them with positive ones:

Prepare ahead of time. Read the lesson before you go to class. Being exposed to the topics that will be covered in class ahead of time, even if you don't understand them perfectly, is extremely helpful in increasing what you retain from the lecture. Do your homework and, if you're still shaky, go over some extra problems. The key to a solid understanding of math is practice.

Sit front and center. When you can easily see and hear, you'll understand more, and you'll avoid the distractions of other students if no one is in front of you. Plus, you're more likely to be sitting with students who are positive and engaged, rather than others with math anxiety. Let their positive math attitude rub off on you.

Ask questions in class and out. If you don't understand something, just ask. If you need a more in-depth explanation, the teacher may need to work with you outside of class, but often it's a simple concept you don't quite understand, and a single question may clear it up. If you wait, you may not be able to follow the rest of the day's lesson. For extra help, most professors have office hours outside of class when you can go over concepts one-on-one to clear up any uncertainties. Additionally, there may be a *math lab* or study session you can attend for homework help. Take advantage of this.

Review. Even if you feel that you've fully mastered a concept, review it periodically to reinforce it. Going over an old lesson has several benefits: solidifying your understanding, giving you a confidence boost, and even giving some new insights into material that you're currently learning! Don't let yourself get rusty. That can lead to problems with learning later concepts.

Teaching Tips

While the math student's mindset is the most crucial to overcoming math anxiety, it is also important for others to adjust their math attitudes. Teachers and parents have an enormous influence on how students relate to math. They can either contribute to math confidence or math anxiety.

As a parent or teacher, it is very important to convey a positive math attitude. Retelling horror stories of your own bad experience with math will contribute to a new generation of math anxiety. Even if you don't share your experiences, others will be able to sense your fears and may begin to believe them.

Even a careless comment can have a big impact, so watch for phrases like *He's not good at math* or *I never liked math*. You are a crucial role model, and your children or students will unconsciously adopt your mindset. Give them a positive example to follow. Rather than teaching them to fear the math world before they even know it, teach them about all its potential and excitement.

Work to present math as an integral, beautiful, and understandable part of life. Encourage creativity in solving problems. Watch for false beliefs and dispel them. Cross the lines between subjects: integrate history, English, and music with math. Show students how math is used every day, and how the entire world is based on mathematical principles, from the pull of gravity to the shape of seashells. Instead of letting students see math as a necessary evil, direct them to view it as an imaginative, beautiful art form – an art form that they are capable of mastering and using.

Don't give too narrow a view of math. It is more than just numbers. Yes, working problems and learning formulas is a large part of classroom math. But don't let the teaching stop there. Teach students about the everyday implications of math. Show them how nature works according to the laws of mathematics, and take them outside to make discoveries of their own. Expose them to math-related careers by inviting visiting speakers, asking students to do research and presentations, and learning students' interests and aptitudes on a personal level.

Demonstrate the importance of math. Many people see math as nothing more than a required stepping stone to their degree, a nuisance with no real usefulness. Teach students that algebra is used every day in managing their bank accounts, in following recipes, and in scheduling the day's events. Show them how learning to do geometric proofs helps them to develop logical thinking, an invaluable life skill. Let them see that math surrounds them and is integrally linked to their daily lives: that weather predictions are based on math, that math was used to design cars and other machines, etc. Most of all, give them the tools to use math to enrich their lives.

Make math as tangible as possible. Use visual aids and objects that can be touched. It is much easier to grasp a concept when you can hold it in your hands and manipulate it, rather than just listening to the lecture. Encourage math outside of the classroom. The real world is full of measuring, counting, and calculating, so let students participate in this. Keep your eyes open for numbers and patterns to discuss. Talk about how scores are calculated in sports games and how far apart plants are placed in a garden row for maximum growth. Build the mindset that math is a normal and interesting part of daily life.

Finally, find math resources that help to build a positive math attitude. There are a number of books that show math as fascinating and exciting while teaching important concepts, for example: *The Math Curse; A Wrinkle in Time; The Phantom Tollbooth;* and *Fractals, Googols and Other Mathematical Tales*. You can also find a number of online resources: math puzzles and games, videos that show math in nature, and communities of math enthusiasts. On a local level, students can compete in a variety of math competitions with other schools or join a math club.

The student who experiences math as exciting and interesting is unlikely to suffer from math anxiety. Going through life without this handicap is an immense advantage and opens many doors that others have closed through their fear.

Self-Check

Whether you suffer from math anxiety or not, chances are that you have been exposed to some of the false beliefs mentioned above. Now is the time to check yourself for any errors you may have accepted. Do you think you're not wired for math? Or that you don't need to understand it since you're not planning on a math career? Do you think math is just too difficult for the average person?

Find the errors you've taken to heart and replace them with positive thinking. Are you capable of learning math? Yes! Can you control your anxiety? Yes! These errors will resurface from time to time, so be watchful. Don't let others with math anxiety influence you or sway your confidence. If you're having trouble with a concept, find help. Don't let it discourage you!

Create a plan of attack for defeating math anxiety and sharpening your skills. Do some research and decide if it would help you to take a class, get a tutor, or find some online resources to fine-tune your knowledge. Make the effort to get good nutrition, hydration, and sleep so that you are operating at full capacity. Remind yourself daily that you are skilled and that anxiety does not control you. Your mind is capable of so much more than you know. Give it the tools it needs to grow and thrive.

Thank You

We at Mometrix would like to extend our heartfelt thanks to you, our friend and patron, for allowing us to play a part in your journey. It is a privilege to serve people from all walks of life who are unified in their commitment to building the best future they can for themselves.

The preparation you devote to these important testing milestones may be the most valuable educational opportunity you have for making a real difference in your life. We encourage you to put your heart into it—that feeling of succeeding, overcoming, and yes, conquering will be well worth the hours you've invested.

We want to hear your story, your struggles and your successes, and if you see any opportunities for us to improve our materials so we can help others even more effectively in the future, please share that with us as well. **The team at Mometrix would be absolutely thrilled to hear from you!** So please, send us an email (support@mometrix.com) and let's stay in touch.

If you'd like some additional help, check out these other resources we offer for your exam:

http://MometrixFlashcards.com/SOL